JESUS OF NAZARETH
in
Word and Deed

JESUS OF NAZARETH
in
Word and Deed

by

Charles C. Cochrane

WILLIAM B. EERDMANS PUBLISHING COMPANY
GRAND RAPIDS, MICHIGAN

Copyright © 1979 by Wm. B. Eerdmans Publishing Co.
255 Jefferson Ave. SE, Grand Rapids, Mich. 49503

Library of Congress Cataloging in Publication Data

Cochrane, Charles C.   1910–
  Jesus of Nazareth in word and deed.

     1.   Jesus Christ—Person and offices.   I.   Title.
BT202.C623   232   78-10804
ISBN 0-8028-1780-7

TO ISOBEL
Donald, William, and Douglas

CONTENTS

Foreword by James I. McCord   ix
Acknowledgements   xi
Introduction   xiii

ONE	The Annunciation	1
TWO	The Anticipation	5
THREE	The Celebration	12
FOUR	The Promise Fulfilled	19
FIVE	The Affirmation	25
SIX	The Acceptance	31
SEVEN	The Declaration	37
EIGHT	The Enlistment	43
NINE	The Devil and the Demons	49
TEN	The Power of Restoration	56
ELEVEN	The Power of Forgiveness	63
TWELVE	The Power to Transform	69
THIRTEEN	The New Freedoms	76
FOURTEEN	Unselfish Service	82
FIFTEEN	Prayer	88
SIXTEEN	The Meaning of Christian Love	95
SEVENTEEN	The Nature of Christian Stewardship	101
EIGHTEEN	The Offering	107
NINETEEN	The Risen Christ	114
TWENTY	Reassurance	121
TWENTY-ONE	The Commission and the Promise	128

FOREWORD

PERIODICALLY IN THE LIFE OF THE CHURCH SOME PARTICULAR
doctrine becomes the focus of concern. Yesterday it was the
God question. Some theologians wrote of the death of God,
while others questioned the legitimacy of any metaphysical language or other supernatural description of the deity. This era has
now passed, but today a new question has arisen, this time about
Jesus Christ. It is posed indirectly by the moratorium on mission
and the fuzzy ambivalence in many churches concerning an appropriate response to the Great Commission. The question of the
Christian faith among other faiths must again be clarified. The
Christological question has been raised directly by a group of
English scholars in the recent volume *The Myth of God Incar-
nate*. Here the issue is whether Jesus of Nazareth claimed to be
divine or whether this is a construction added by the early
Church.

Dr. Charles C. Cochrane, a distinguished minister in the Presbyterian Church in Canada, has made a valuable contribution in
this vital area in *Jesus of Nazareth in Word and Deed*. This does
not mean that the author has deliberately responded to the questions posed above. Rather, his intention in this volume is "to see
our Lord's ministry whole." Basing his chapters primarily on the
Gospels of Mark and Luke, he develops the career of Jesus from
the Annunciation through the Commission and the promise of
the Spirit. For him the theme of the Bible is God's relentless
pursuit of the sinner, culminating in the reconciling mission of
Jesus Christ. Rejecting "cheap grace," the author shows how the
old and the new age overlap, and takes seriously the ambiguities

and struggles that continue to characterize human life and history.

The charge is often lodged that Reformed theology does not give enough attention to the redeemed life. A strength of this book is its emphasis on stewardship, prayer, and Christian witness. Throughout each chapter there is evidence of an able and concerned pastor who is well-grounded in theology and who knows and cares about his people.

In a period of doubt and confusion, when so many sermons reflect little more than pop psychology, it is a joy to read and commend a volume of sermonic essays that are solidly Biblical and theological and, at the same time, are related to the problems and challenges the Christian faces every day. Word and deed conjoined produce witness, as Jesus of Nazareth bore witness to His Father when "the Word became flesh and dwelt among us." Reading this volume will be a stimulus to us to bear witness in our lives to Him who now reigns as Lord of life and of death.

James I. McCord, President
Princeton Theological Seminary

ACKNOWLEDGEMENTS

IT IS RARELY THE CASE IN AN ENTERPRISE OF THIS KIND THAT one individual is solely responsible for the completed work, though it may bear his name. Accordingly, I wish to express my thanks and deep appreciation to Dr. Norman F. Langford of Philadelphia whose invaluable advice—both theological and literary—has contributed greatly to any merit the book may be said to possess; to Dr. James I. McCord of Princeton Theological Seminary for graciously consenting to provide a Foreword to this series of expositions; and to Dr. Arthur C. Cochrane, formerly of Dubuque and Pittsburgh Theological Seminaries respectively, and presently special lecturer at Wartburg Lutheran College, also in Dubuque, whose warm fraternal encouragement is responsible for its being offered to the general public.

Finally, I am deeply indebted to my former congregation— Melville Presbyterian Church, Montreal, Canada—for their generous patience with a minister who seemed, for long periods of time, to be closeted in his Study.

Charles C. Cochrane

The Tri-congregations
Toronto, Canada

INTRODUCTION

THE PURPOSE OF THIS MODEST VOLUME IS TO SET FORTH AN orderly statement of who Jesus of Nazareth was and is which will prove intelligible to the learner and the learned alike. To do this, I have chosen the Gospels of Mark and Luke as primary sources, with such confirmation from other biblical sources as may be required for clear understanding. The selection of circumstances and incidents recorded in these Gospels has been made with a view to our main theme: to enunciate in a manner faithful to the New Testament the identity of Jesus "who is called Christ." A few introductory observations about our primary sources may therefore not be out of place.

If the dates usually ascribed to the Gospels of Mark and Luke are even approximately correct, a full generation had passed since the death and resurrection of our Lord. During that time many of those who had witnessed his life, death, and resurrection had died, and doubtless many had been martyred. Accordingly, the time was bound to come when no eyewitnesses would be left to record the events of Jesus' life and ministry for future genera-tions. This is a motive shared by all four Evangelists in putting the gospel record in writing. Each wrote from his own point of view, with his own particular concerns before him, and his own constituency of readers in mind—using the best sources available to him.

All four Gospels teach that Jesus was the Messiah—the Son of God and the Savior of the world. Yet there are some distinctions to be made between the Gospels. Unlike Luke, Mark did not begin his record of Jesus' ministry with a prologue setting forth his reason for writing. We believe, however, that we are able to discern his purpose with some accuracy from the content of the Gospel itself, and by taking note of the needs of the people for whom it was originally intended. It is generally conceded that Mark wrote especially for the Christians settled in Rome. The most recent scholarship dates the writing of this Gospel between A.D. 65 and 75; the infamous Roman Emperor Nero reigned from A.D. 54 to 68. The Christian community had been mercilessly persecuted and tortured by this madman; and Mark was writing to strengthen a church under oppression and apparently destined for martyrdom.

Under such immediately pressing circumstances, Mark might not wish to dwell at length on the incarnation, theories of the atonement, details of the empty tomb, nor indeed on Jesus' childhood. He would be more likely to write of Jesus' ministry, death, and resurrection—and of how to be a faithful disciple in times of adversity. Mark shows that the way of Jesus was the way of the cross, and that this way must still be followed. It requires renunciation, bearing one's burdens, losing one's life to save it, and serving others. Jesus did not demand of others more than he gave of himself. For those who might wonder why Jesus died as he did, Mark, as early as the second chapter, shows that Jesus died because he was hated and distrusted by the religious leaders, and because it was the Father's will that he die "for many."

According to Mark it was only in the later stages of his ministry that Jesus claimed to be the Messiah. Jesus was at first deliberately reticent, fearing perhaps a profound misunderstanding of his role as having political and nationalistic overtones. The crowds, and even the disciples, were unbelievably obtuse considering what they heard and saw. Whatever the answer may be, there is no doubt that Mark presents our Lord as carefully preserving his divine anonymity almost to the end (see, for example, Mark 1:34; 5:43; and even 15:2–5). This has led some scholars to speak of the "Messianic secret," which they associate chiefly with Mark's presentation—namely, that Jesus deliberately took care that his true identity not be known.

What are we to make of this? May there not be a very good theological reason for Jesus' reluctance to let the public know his identity? There is strong evidence that Jesus did not want even his own disciples to believe that he was the Messiah simply because he told them so; and this would naturally apply to others as well. A case in point is the incident involving John and his disciples (Matt. 11:2–5) in which Jesus' answer was very far from being a direct "yes" or "no." Our Lord appears to be saying, "On the basis of what you hear and see, the decision is yours." It is at least conceivable, considering the profound and intense loyalty Jesus evoked, that he could have induced great numbers of people to believe in him by telling them so directly, by making his claim public and persuasive. He refrained from exerting any personal pressure which would tend to deprive his listeners of the privilege, freedom, and responsibility of making their own decision. In this connection we may be permitted to hear an echo of Paul's teaching to the effect that Christian faith rests not "in the wisdom of men but in the power of God" (1 Cor. 2). It seems not unlikely that in seeking to protect the "Messianic secret" Jesus was giving place to the Holy Spirit who would one day lead the disciples "into all truth" (John 16:13).

*   *   *

Luke's purpose in writing his account of the gospel is set down in the opening verses. It was to write a plain yet mature statement of the historical events on which the faith is based. Having, as we would say, "examined all the sources," he would lay before Theophilus an orderly presentation of the material that his friend had already received in a somewhat disjointed form. (The suggestion has been made, and cannot altogether be dismissed, that Theophilus, rather than being a friend of Luke, was a person of eminence whose influence Luke wanted to enlist for the protection of the Christian community. In this event Luke would wish to assure Theophilus that the gospel would neither undermine the social fabric nor subvert the political process.)

The book is sometimes referred to as the Gentile Christian Gospel because there are reasons for believing that the author had the Gentile community primarily in mind. It is to be noted, for example, that Luke traces Jesus' ancestry to Adam rather than to Abraham, indicating that God's plan of salvation is not confined to the Jews alone; that in the song of Simeon the infant Jesus is hailed as "a light for revelation to the Gentiles"; that the Samaritans, almost proverbially at odds with the Jews, are twice singled out for praise; that a Gentile centurion is made the prototype of all Gentiles who will subsequently believe; and that the "good news" shall be preached to "all nations."

ONE

THE ANNUNCIATION

Mark 1:1-3 _____ Luke 1:1-38

THE BIRTHS OF JOHN AND JESUS RESPECTIVELY WERE AN-nounced beforehand. The point here is that these were not "ordi-nary" births, the great majority of which go unheralded. We are to understand, rather, that these are events of the greatest impor-tance in God's over-all plan for humanity. It had been so, for example, in earlier times with Abram and Sarai. Past the age when she might expect to bear a child, she would nevertheless receive a son. So the announcement said, and so it was; and Isaac became the second generation of the people of God in his day (see esp. Gen. 17 and 21). It was the same when Samuel was born, for Hannah too was barren. Yet she so desired a child of her own that she wept bitterly and prayed constantly that the Lord would remove her "affliction." Eli the priest privately heralded the birth of Samuel; and it was Samuel who from earliest childhood was first a servant and then a prophet of the Lord. And this happened at a time in Israel's history when "the word of the Lord was rare" (1 Sam. 3:1).

Heralded, miraculous birth is, according to the biblical wit-ness, a direct sign that God is about to intervene creatively on behalf of his people Israel. Two such events, so close to one another in time as to overlap, may be said to signal an interven-tion of truly cosmic proportions. As one writer has observed, Luke so arranged his material as to bring out the theological message. The births of John the Baptist and of Jesus are carefully related in such a way that the pattern of both is the same, with only minor variations. Both follow the birth, circumcision, man-ifestation sequence; and both "grew and became strong" (Luke

1:80; 2:40). The contrasts, too, are striking. Zechariah reacted negatively to the announcement (1:18) and was mildly punished for his unbelief; Mary accepted the news with wonder and joy (1:38). John will be great *before God*; Jesus will be great without qualification (note that in the Psalms, *God* is called great). John's mission was temporary, preparatory; Jesus' mission was eternal.

The language used and the references chosen from the Old Testament are further evidence that Luke regards the birth of Jesus as the dawn of the Messianic age. In Daniel it is the angel Gabriel who predicts that there are seventy weeks until the coming of "everlasting righteousness" (9:24), and it is Gabriel again who announces in effect that "the new age" has dawned in the birth of Jesus. (The elapsed time from the announcement to Zechariah to the presentation of Jesus in the Temple is 490 days; i.e. 70 weeks.) Much of Luke 1:16ff seems to be derived from Malachi 3 and 4. The messenger referred to by Malachi as preparing the way for God is now identified as John the Baptist, who will prepare the way for Jesus. In Malachi the Lord will appear suddenly in his Temple; in Luke 2:22–35 Jesus appears there. The glory of the Lord which "filled the tent of meeting" (Exod. 40:35) is seen by the eyes of Simeon (Luke 2:32).

The mature and painstaking judgment of Luke, writing some eighty years after the event, is that this child Jesus is indeed the promised Messiah of God, and he so chooses his words and contexts as to make it as clear as is humanly possible.

         🔥   *   ❀

One of the most engaging aspects of the birth stories of John and Jesus is the utter simplicity of both the narratives and the people involved. There is no trace of an appeal to prestige in the respective annunciations. And even when we learn that Zechariah was a priest and Elizabeth of a priestly family, it is not said in the manner of those who later boasted that "we have Abraham to our father" (Luke 3:8). Instead we find Zechariah going about his priestly (and somewhat menial?) duties of burning incense to rid the Temple of the stench of sacrificial animals. And it is noted that they were both "righteous before God, walking in all the commandments and ordinances of the Lord blameless." If there is a characteristic common to the principals of these stories, it must surely be humility. These two devout, unpretentious people were to be honored by God in becoming the parents of John the Baptist.

The structure of the Israelite nation in the early times was by tribe, family, and "house"—much as medieval society among the Hungarians and Celts (particularly in the highlands of Scotland) was organized according to clans, septs, and families. Thus Joseph was of the house and lineage (family) of David (2:4), and of the tribe of Judah. But even this smidgen of information is not included to enhance the family and person of our Lord; there were doubtless many in Israel for whom a similar claim could be made. It is, rather, a simple notation, twice repeated, that Jesus' lineage conforms to the prophecy that the Messiah would spring from the tribe of Judah. Despite the intimations of royalty in Jesus' ancestry, the family into which he was born was essentially a modest one, Joseph being a carpenter by trade. Of Mary we know little with certainty, though some scholars believe that she too was of Davidic origin.

*　　　*　　　*

Picture if you will the faithful Zechariah, no longer a young man, pursuing the even tenor of his priestly ways in the Temple. Upon one such occasion there "appeared" to him the figure of an angel. Zechariah's reaction was more than mere surprise—it was fear. "What have I done?" "What have I omitted to do?" These two questions may have entered his mind. On the other hand, he may have been alarmed beyond the possibility of rational thought, "frightened stiff" as we sometimes say. The incident is not unique in Scripture.

In any event, what we have to learn here is that it is one and the same God who hurts and heals us, who brings both fear and comfort, joy and sadness. There is no other. The angel's sole credential is that he stands "in the presence of God"—the same God whom Zechariah serves. The moment is not therefore one for dread and fear but for praise and rejoicing. Gabriel has not come on a mission of judgment, but to deliver good news.

We have seen that Zechariah was an exemplary Jew, walking

in the commandments of the Lord "blameless." That is high praise indeed. Then we are told that he "did not believe my words." Blameless? Yes. Perfect? No. The Bible will not permit us to idealize the men and women who appear on its pages. But what a beautifully accurate description of the frailty and imperfection of human nature! How readily we, similarly afflicted, may recognize our own shortcomings in the faults of even so steadfast a man as Zechariah!

TWO

THE ANTICIPATION

1 Samuel 2:1–10 ——————————————— Luke 1:39–79

IT HAS OFTEN BEEN SAID THAT SCRIPTURE, IN MANY OF ITS
teachings, is "unsatisfactory" because it does not answer all our
questions, explain all our difficulties, and resolve all our problems. It has also been suggested, in rebuttal, that perhaps we are
so anxious to have *our* questions answered that we do not wait to
hear what Scripture wants to tell *us*. It is just possible that if we
were to listen carefully as we read, we would find many of the
questions in our minds unnecessary.

The first seven verses of our New Testament reference might
bring to mind a number of questions. What was the name of the
"city of Judah" where Zechariah and Elizabeth lived? Why did
Mary leave Nazareth to visit her kinswoman? With what words
did Mary greet Elizabeth? How, without any explanation, was
Elizabeth able to identify Mary as "the mother of my Lord?"
And what are we to make of the unborn babe (John) leaping in
the womb in the presence of the mother-to-be of Christ the King?

These are questions to which Luke has given no answer. We
may feel that some of them are partially answered in that
Elizabeth herself was no stranger to the miraculous works of
God; and secondly, we note the all-important statement that
Elizabeth "was filled with the Holy Spirit." In general, however,
we may understand that both Elizabeth and Mary believed, with
little or no supporting evidence, that the things which God had
promised from the beginning he was now about to accomplish.
Or again, it may well be that Luke's silence is more significant
than anything he could say; and that even the faith of Elizabeth
and Mary is entirely the work of God.

If that is the case, then those of us who approach Scripture in order to have *our* questions answered (and who does not?) have the tables turned on us, and it is we who are being questioned: Do we also believe? We face the undoubted fact that faith in God is a mystery. Faith may be described in many ways. The confident awareness of the presence of God shared by Jacob as he wrestled with him (Gen. 32:24ff), by Job while he argued with him (e.g. 2:10), by Jonah even as he disobeyed him (3:1-3), and by Habakkuk when stripped of all he possessed (3:17f). To have faith is to believe God for his own sake regardless of local conditions, with no supporting evidence, and sometimes, against one's "better judgment." It is the faith spoken of by the nineteenth-century hymn-writer J. S. B. Monsell:

> *Only believe, and thou shalt see*
> *That Christ is all in all to thee.*

The sequence here is correct: faith precedes understanding.

This is not to say that there is no evidence. There is plenty of it, and we are encouraged "always to be prepared to make a defense to anyone who calls you to account for the hope that is in you" (1 Peter 3:15). But Luke was not making a defense; he was telling a story—a story which has become part of your defense, and mine.

*　　　　*　　　　*

In keeping with the will of God as told her by the angel, and in her submission to it ("let it be to me according to your word"), Mary accepts her situation, exults in it, and is grateful for it. As might be expected, the Magnificat is more personal than the song of Zechariah. Mary marvels at God's gracious condescension that she of humble station had become so uniquely the object of divine favor. Like Abraham (Gen. 22:18), she is confident that "all generations" will regard her as singularly blessed. In all of this Mary recognizes the fulfillment of God's promise and purpose in having called Abraham and in having created a people.

It might easily have been otherwise with Mary. Had the course of events been ordinary, and Mary faced with the prospect of bearing an uninvited child, her lot would have been one of disgrace and shame. (Perhaps, indeed, it was so, throughout her pregnancy and Jesus' early life. We do not know; the only indication we have of public attitudes is in Joseph's willingness in Matthew 1:19 to annul their promise of marriage.) It is therefore the more remarkable that Mary accepted her role as she did, not with resignation and resentment, but with joy and gladness. We can comprehend Mary's attitude only in the light of her evident familiarity with the traditions of her people, her awareness of the Messianic expectation of Israel, and the presence of God's Holy Spirit in her heart.

In connection with Zechariah's song (the Benedictus) we again find the all-important statement: "Zechariah was filled with the Holy Spirit"; that is, God is at work in Zechariah's confession (as he is in ours). Zechariah's punitive silence has come to an end as promised by the angel Gabriel. Zechariah, having all his life rendered faithful obedience to God now also *believes* him, and accordingly has something to say. The word "Benedictus," given as a title to Zechariah's song, is from the first word of the song in the Latin Vulgate—a translation of the Bible made by St. Jerome in A.D. 385.

In Zechariah's song of praise and thanksgiving the same insights are apparent as in the Magnificat, but are seen from a different point of view. God's intervention is for "his people," for "the house of his servant David"; it is a mercy promised "to our fathers," and conforms to the words spoken "by the mouth of his holy prophets." In this way, nationally, does Zechariah understand and rejoice at the impending birth of Mary's child. His own newly born son will be the prophet (herald) of this event. From the beginning John's role will be subordinate to that of Jesus, as he himself later declared: "He must increase, but I must decrease" (John 3:30).

Whether or not the Benedictus originated spontaneously with Zechariah, it is nevertheless a passage of exceptional beauty, brevity, and cohesiveness. It expresses, within the compass of a few words, the joy and exultation of a faithful Jew upon finding that the God whom he has worshiped and served all his life has chosen this moment, that is, his own lifetime, to reveal his faithfulness. If we find that many of the phrases used in the Benedictus have been used before, we should not be surprised.

Indeed it is what we might expect. The church does the same thing in its hymns and prayers and selections from the Psalter—and excerpts too from the finest prayers of the early Christians. Zechariah's use of the language of adoration in the tradition of his own people is a measure of his familiarity with it. For possible sources, see Psalms 41:13; 105:8f; 106:10; 111:9; 132:17; and Micah 7:20.

*   *   *

To a modern reader of the Gospel, the discussion provoked by the choice of a name for Elizabeth's child may seem to have been nothing more than a "tempest in a tea-pot," a passing incident of no real importance. Parents give their children particular names for a variety of reasons: to honor a friend or relative, to mark a day, date, or event, to maintain the continuity of the generations, or simply because the name is pleasing. Although many English names have meanings, they are seldom chosen for that reason.

In biblical times it was not so; the meaning of a name was of primary importance (as may be seen from the number of definitions given in the margins of many versions of the Bible), and the choosing of it was much less casual.

The creation of new life is a never-ending source of wonderment and fascination, and the diminutive of any species never fails to attract attention. Accordingly, at the birth and circumcision of Elizabeth's baby the neighbors and kinsfolk gathered around, even as we do today. Luke has a good story here and he tells it with restraint, dignity, and reverence. This is the only place in Scripture which supports the view that the name of the child was given at the time of circumcision, but Luke can scarcely have been wrong. Apparently the guests took it for granted that the child, being the first-born, would be given his father's name, or at least the name of a relative. This would have been entirely appropriate: Zechariah means "God has remembered"; there are more than thirty Zechariahs mentioned in the Bible; and the continuity of the generations would have been maintained. Elizabeth, however, objected: "He shall be called John," recalling, of course, the instruction of the angel (v. 13). The guests made the usual protests, and appealed to the father for his view. Zechariah did not give them "his view"; he wrote, "His name *is* John." This too is appropriate: John (Hebrew, Yohanan) means "God has been gracious," as indeed he had. When Elizabeth and Zechariah confirmed the instruction of the angel in naming their baby John, it was not merely a matter of obedience. These two faithful people were saying "Amen" to the statement made by John's name.

The neighbors were, to say the least, impressed. They had celebrated the birth and witnessed the circumcision of a child to whom God, not the parents, had given a name. It was "the talk of the town" (v. 65). What was so special about this child? A little more than two decades would pass before they would know the answer for themselves.

*   *   *

The Israelites are a unique people, different from all other peoples of the world. Israel's uniqueness does not consist in the characteristics of the people who bear the name; in all other respects but one they are much the same as their contemporaries in any age. They do not even constitute a race; they belong, as do several others, to the Semites. They are a "people" within a race.

The singularity of the Israelites may be found in the relationship between the people and their God—a relationship which is established and defined by the word "covenant." To say that God "chose" Israel, though true, can be misleading. It is not as though God, looking down as it were upon the nations of the earth, chose one of them to be his people. Rather, in choosing he created, and in creating he chose. He brought Israel into being by virtue of his covenant with Abraham (Gen. 12:1–3), and by the renewal of that covenant with Isaac and Jacob and with Jacob's sons, who became the heads of the twelve tribes of Israel.

The covenant God made with Abraham and his descendants was unique in that it was indestructible. On God's side it was the nature of a promise: "I will bless you . . . so that you will be a blessing"; on Israel's part it required obedience: "if you will obey my voice and keep my covenant you will be my own possession among all peoples" (Exod. 19:5f). Nevertheless, Israel's sub-

–9–

sequent acts of disobedience and apostasy did not annul the covenant. God remained faithful, whether or not Israel did the same.

To be God's people—his elect, his chosen—is no small consideration. It suggests favoritism based on outstanding merit or virtue, and therefore a status of privilege. But Israel learned differently; the call of God is a call to obedience, to service, and frequently to suffering. Sometimes the people of Israel would forget what they had learned. In times of prosperity they would lay it to their own account; in adversity it would be said that God had deserted them. Thus the intensity of their conviction of being God's people waxed and waned with the passing of the years, yet at no time was it completely extinguished, and the hope born of God's promise was never entirely abandoned.

At the time of Jesus' birth it must have seemed to thoughtful Jews that all they had to cling to was hope. With the single exception of the reigns of David and Solomon, the centuries had brought them reversals, captivities, dispersions, and subjugation. Yesterday it had been Assyria or Babylonia or Greece, and today it was Rome. Would God, *their* God, never intervene and set his people free? Would God's anointed never come?

Now let us go back, very briefly, to the terms of God's original promise. God had said to Abraham—and corporately to his descendants—"I will bless you and make your name great." God's blessing is the expression of his favor, his mercy, and his grace. But the sentence does not stop there: ". . . so that you will be a blessing" (to others). God's covenant is *with* Israel, and *for* all people (Luke 2:10). Others are also to receive a blessing, and Israel will be God's chosen vehicle from which that blessing will emerge.

In view of Israel's long history of disappointment, frustration, and frequent oppression, it is not remarkable that in the interpretation of the Messianic expectation the emphasis should fall on the first part of God's promise rather than on the second. According to the popular view, the Messiah would be a national hero, a liberator who would vindicate the Jews in the eyes (and at the expense?) of neighboring states. Surely, a first order of business would be to rid Palestine of the humiliating presence of the Roman masters.

As we read about Jesus, watching and listening through the

eyes and ears of the evangelists, it becomes more and more apparent that he had little in common with the popular view.. Rather, he seemed to draw on the description of the Suffering Servant (Isa. 53) as his guide and inspiration. Overcoming the Romans did not seem of first importance to him whose task was to overcome the world (John 16:33).

THREE

THE CELEBRATION

Luke 2:1-20 _____

THE BIRTHS OF ISAAC TO ABRAHAM AND SARAH, OF SAMUEL to Elkanah and Hannah, and of John to Zechariah and Elizabeth were miraculous, but not altogether unique. According to Luke the birth of Jesus to Mary was both miraculous *and* unique. Its uniqueness is couched in terms of a "virgin birth." The ground for this teaching has already been laid in the first chapter by Mary's question, "How can this be, since I have no husband?" and by the angel's reply, "The Holy Spirit will come upon you . . ." (vv. 34, 35).

In a later chapter we will examine more fully the meaning of the word "miracle" as it is used in the New Testament. There we will learn that miracles are not introduced to test our credulity; they are signs of the power of the new age that dawned in the coming of the Savior. More particularly, they are signs of God's sovereign, active presence in the event, of God's dynamic intervention in human history. According to the biblical witness there was no natural possibility of Sarah, Hannah, or Elizabeth giving birth to a baby. That they did so points to miracle, and miracle points to God. Thus the church has traditionally believed and taught that Jesus' birth is a sign of the incarnation, or as John expressed it: "the Word became flesh and dwelt among us."

*   *   *

In view of the immensity of the claim made for the birth of Jesus by Luke (with Matthew), it is not altogether surprising that questions have been raised about its historical reality as a truly

virgin birth. This is particularly true in an age of rapid advancement in literary criticism and scientific knowledge, and in an era
of self-conscious sophistication. It is pointed out that Isaiah's
prophecy (7:14) is more accurately translated "a young woman
shall conceive..." than "a virgin shall conceive..."; hence we
are not tied to a doctrine of virgin birth by Old Testament
prophecy. Again, it is said that by nature a virgin birth is both
unnatural and impossible. It has also been observed that neither
Mark nor John records a birth story and both seem unaware of the
claim; and finally, that nowhere in his letters does Paul even
mention it. Though fully aware that a matter of this kind will not
be settled by arguments "for" and "against"—articles of faith are
never resolved by majority vote—we would be most remiss to
ignore the question entirely.

With respect to the correct translation of the phrase in Isaiah,
it may be conceded that the expression "young woman" does not
preclude the possibility of her being a virgin. Secondly, nothing
is to be gained in terms of the propagation of the supra-natural
gospel by excluding the possibility of a supra-natural birth. Having just read Luke 1:37, it is difficult to reject the virgin birth on
the grounds that it is impossible (see also Mark 10:27, 14:36; and
Luke 18:27). Further, the argument from silence (of Mark and
John) is hardly impressive. If, as is sometimes supposed, Mark
was ignorant of the virgin birth, it is surprising that he referred
to Jesus as "the son of Mary" (6:3) rather than, in accordance
with normal Jewish usage, "the son of Joseph." In similar vein
Matthew can tell the same story and call him "the carpenter's
son" without fear of misunderstanding, since he has included a
birth story. Finally, Paul does not proclaim the virgin birth. Was
he unaware of it? His reference to Christ as "the last Adam" may
suggest not only that he is the first-born of many brethren—the
new humanity—but also that neither the first Adam nor the
second owes his existence to a human father.

At least as many problems are raised by rejecting the teaching
of the virgin birth as by accepting it. We would, for example,
have completely to reassess the validity of the prologue to Luke's
Gospel—in particular his claim to have "followed all things
closely" and "to write an orderly account" (Luke 1:3). Or again,
the "argument from silence" (of Mark and John) poses the ques-

tion, If there was a virgin birth why do they not include birth stories in their Gospels? But an even more difficult question arises: If there was *no* virgin birth why do Matthew and Luke say there was? It seems most unlikely that the first and third evangelists would present the Christian community with a fabricated story of virgin birth to support what that community already believed—the incarnation.

Matthew (1:23), in providing a translation of Jesus' name (Emmanuel: God with us), has gone directly to the heart of the matter. This is the broad meaning of the Savior's birth: that God is with us. James Sanders has called him "the God who goes calling." He dropped in on our first parents "in the garden in the cool of the day"; he interrupted Moses gazing at the burning bush; he disturbed Samuel, at first anonymously, just as the young lad was trying to get some sleep; he diverted Amos "from following the flock," and so it was with a host of others. In Jesus Christ God has come to his people, not to visit but to stay. He has come in person—in the person of his Son. Certain ones who witnessed the raising of the son of the widow of Nain recognized his presence for what it was, and exclaimed: "God has visited his people!" (Luke 7:16). It was not as clear then as it would be later that Jesus planned to be with us "always, to the close of the age" (Matt. 28:20).

*　　　　　*　　　　　*

Luke fixes the time of the birth of Jesus with a two-fold reference: the reign of Augustus Caesar, and Quirinius' governorship of Syria. By placing the event in the context of human history the evangelist seems to be saying, "this is not folklore, this is fact."

We know that the passage of about 2000 years separated the lives of Abraham and Jesus, and that a similar period has elapsed since the life of Jesus to the present day. So much for chronological sequence. Paul has a different way of telling us when the Word became flesh. He left a note behind addressed to the Galatian churches (4:4) which reads as follows: "But when the time had fully come, God sent forth his Son, born of a woman. . . ." This is a perfectly delightful phrase because it is so completely satisfying; and it puts the "timing" well out of reach of our presumptions and prejudices. Why did not God bring forth his Son a thousand years earlier? Answer: because the time had not fully come. Did God wait for the world to become so evil that there was no alternative but to send a Savior? No hint of that appears in Scripture. Did God choose a time of which it might be said that his people had achieved an acceptable standard of righteousness? No; not that either. "When the time had fully come" means quite simply, "When it pleased God to do so." There is no compulsion of circumstances or events which would limit God's perfect freedom; Christ's birth was supremely an act of grace that took place at a time of God's own choosing.

When we have accepted the fact that God sent forth his Son in the freedom of his own will, we may then note certain factors favorable to the spread of the gospel. The Jews had already, through exile in Babylonia, had some experience of living away from their homeland in Palestine. At the beginning of the third century B.C. thousands of Jews were taken to Egypt as colonists, and at about the same time the influence of the Greek language and culture was brought to bear on Palestine from two great centers—Alexandria and Antioch. The Jews during these times had also learned to trade, and the opportunities for "worldwide" traffic in goods, which Alexander's conquests had made for the Greeks, attracted the Jews also. Finally, the rise of the Roman Empire, which included the building of roads for Roman armies, vastly increased the mobility of the people. As is evident from Acts 2:5-11, by New Testament times there were settlements of Jews in nearly every major city in the Mediterranean area. With the Jews went their synagogues; and to the synagogues went, originally, the bearers of the gospel.

*　　　　　*　　　　　*

Everything about the birth, life, and death of Jesus speaks of humility and is calculated to exclude pride. To such an extent is this true that it can only have been deliberate. Consider, for example, the people from whom Jesus sprang at birth—surely not the most illustrious nation on earth at the time. They had had only one brief "golden age"—that of David and Solomon—as we normally view these periods of ascendancy. They lacked the power and the glamor of the Persians, the Assyrians, and the Egyptians; and their land had been overrun by each in turn. They did not have the learning of the Greeks or the military prowess of the Romans. When God promised Abraham (Gen. 12:3) to make of him "a great nation," that promise implied none of the usual attributes of fame and eminence. It meant great *before God*. In the changing national fortunes of Egypt, Assyria, and Babylonia, Palestine (like Belgium during the two World Wars) was a land that had to be traversed for the rival armies of the great powers to meet in mortal combat. Geography had placed Israel at the crossroads of many struggles for military ascendancy, and made them participants in wars that were not of their own choosing. The distinction that set Israel apart from other nations was not commonly regarded as a source of pride. In short, if God had wanted to introduce his Son in circumstances of worldly eminence, he could have chosen Greek or Roman parentage and environment to greater advantage.

Joseph and Mary were in no respect an exceptional couple. They were not particularly gifted, politically prominent, or financially endowed. They were ordinary people. The Bible does teach that they were people of character, integrity, and religious conviction (Matt. 1:19; Luke 1:38). But it is not recorded that they were even close to the top of the social ladder.

The circumstances of the birth itself render comment almost superfluous. We have observed already that Nazareth was a village of no particular note. Residence there would scarcely enhance the reputation of a celebrity. Neither was the situation in Bethlehem which resulted in Jesus being born in a barn conducive to pride of birth.

What does all this mean? In a later chapter we will have occasion to observe that in the New Testament the priorities, criteria, and standards of the world are consistently rejected and reversed. It is not merely a frequent thing: it is a fundamental denial of the values to which we normally adhere and regard as important. No more conspicuous example of the contrast between the new age and the old, between the kingdom of God and the kingdoms of this world, can be found than in the sequence of events and conditions surrounding the birth of the Christ-child.

Pomp and circumstance, fame and riches, power and prestige are ignored; and in their place, as of first importance, are love, patience, obedience, faithfulness, integrity, and humility. This is appropriate in connection with the birth of the One who would later warn (Luke 16:15) that "what is exalted among men is an abomination in the sight of God," and who would teach that "everyone who exalts himself will be humbled, and he who humbles himself will be exalted" (Luke 14:11; 18:14).

The gospel's radical reassessment of human values begins with the Savior's birth.

*   *   *

The intense fear of the shepherds when visited in the darkness without prior warning was doubtless in proportion to the brilliance of the display which accompanied the announcement of the birth. We know now that there was no reason for their fear, but would we have known it then? Would we have reacted differently? When God intervenes graciously our fear is but for a moment. It seems to have been so with the shepherds. It is in mercy, not judgment, that the angel comes to them. The Davidic king is born. The news is "good," yet its majestic grandeur is still concealed from human understanding. In spite of the celestial fanfare, the royal birth takes place in a cattle stall. The angels and the heavenly host exalt him now; humanity will exalt him later. "Glory to God in the highest, and on earth peace among men with whom he is pleased."

The angels leave, and the shepherds—their fears allayed—confer. Their interest has been aroused and their curiosity piqued. They would go to Bethlehem to see for themselves. Many of us come to Christian faith in somewhat the same way. On one occasion a young man joined a Christian group on campus, not because he believed, but to learn something of this Jesus of whom his friends spoke with such enthusiasm and reverence. His interest had been stirred, and because he had had no previous contact with Christian faith he wanted to find out for himself. Today he is a deeply committed Christian.

The shepherds went "with haste"—perhaps in their eager desire to see the infant Jesus; perhaps so as not to leave the sheep untended for too long. Returning to their work "glorifying and praising God," the shepherds were among the first of those men, women, and children who down through the years have "exalted the Word." What they began we continue, and those who come after us will perpetuate to the end of time.

*   *   *

It is rather a neat turn of phrase to say that "Mary kept all these things and pondered them in her heart." Many women have doubtless done so, but Mary had more to ponder than most. "All these things"—all that had transpired since the angel's original message: God choosing her to be his "handmaiden"; Joseph's quiet dignity and faithfulness; the shepherds' report of what they had learned while tending the flock; and, of course, Jesus, her child, the Son of God. Perhaps Mary could not quite understand the meaning of it all; but from the outset (1:38) she had placed herself completely in God's hands, and there is no suggestion that she wished it otherwise.

The birth of Jesus brought joy to Joseph and Mary, to Zechariah and Elizabeth, to the shepherds in the field, to "the multitude of the heavenly host," to Simeon and Anna, and, as related by Matthew, to the Wise Men. It did not, however, bring joy to Herod. Poor Herod! He thought that Jesus had come to take something (his throne) away from him. He did not know that Jesus had come to give him something infinitely more precious than all he possessed.

Christmas joy is our grateful response to God, who, through the gift of his Son, has restored our lives and become our salvation.

FOUR
THE PROMISE FULFILLED

Luke 2:21–28 _____

ENGLISH WORDS OFTEN HAVE MORE THAN ONE MEANING
and are used in more than one context. "Prophecy" (and its
related noun "prophet" and verb "prophesy") is one such word.
Thus it may be useful at the outset to make some distinctions to
avoid the possibility of misunderstandings. In its popular use
prophecy is sometimes equated with prediction, such that to
prophesy is to predict, to foretell future events. But when the
Scriptures of the Old Testament are regarded solely as a collection of predictions, a very great disservice is done to our understanding of it. Seen in this light it takes on some of the characteristics of magic, even of the occult. And even more important,
we may become so obsessed with the element of prediction that
we fail to hear what God wants to tell us.

Prophecy, in the biblical sense, is an authoritative statement
or expression of God's will for his people. It is frequently preceded by the words: "Thus says the Lord." The prophet is not the
source of the message, but merely its vehicle. He is not giving his
opinion, but declaring God's will. As one writer has pointed out,
to substitute "thus thinks the prophet" for "thus says the Lord"
is very like playing *Hamlet* without the Prince of Denmark.

The genuine prophet of the Old Testament is never self-
appointed. Moses, upon being called, sought, rather than assumed, authority for his mission (see Exod. 3:11); Jeremiah
balked at being a prophet on the grounds of his youth (1:6); and
Amos told Amaziah that he had had no interest in prophesying
until the Lord took him from following the flock (7:14). From the
experiences of these men and others, it is plain that it is God
himself who chooses his prophets, and he qualifies them for this

office by putting his words on their lips. "I will raise up for them a prophet like you from among their brethren; and I will put my words in his mouth, and he shall speak to them all that I command him" (Deut. 18:18). The words given to the prophet are irresistible, and try as he may he cannot but proclaim them. "There is in my heart as it were a burning fire shut up in my bones, and I am weary with holding it in, and I cannot" (Jer. 20:9). "The Lord God has spoken; who can but prophesy?" (Amos 3:8). God authenticated his word on their lips. "They made their hearts like adamant lest they should hear the law and the words which the Lord of hosts has sent by his spirit through the former prophets. Therefore great wrath came from the Lord of hosts" (Zech. 7:12).

Once we have made the necessary distinction between prophecy and prediction, we may go back and note that prophecy frequently *included* prediction. "Go and say to Hezekiah ... I will add fifteen years to your life ... I will deliver you and this city out of the hand of the king of Assyria and defend this city" (Isa. 38:5, 6). "Behold, the days are coming when all that is in your house and that which your fathers have stored up till this day will be carried to Babylon" (Isa. 39:5). But by far the greater part of a prophet's work concerned the past and the present: reminding the community that they were uniquely God's people—the people of God's promise; and calling them back to faithfulness of heart to the one God, and to the high standard of ethical purity required of them.

The Old Testament material which bears directly on the Messianic expectation—and gave rise to it—has to do with the past, the present, and the future. It contains elements of both prophecy and prediction. The prophecy is derived from the promise made originally to Abraham and perpetuated through his descendants. It is reiterated from generation to generation, reminding the people of the faithfulness of the God who created them. And in reminding the people of the past and speaking to them in the present, the Old Testament also looks ahead to the day of the Lord in which the Messiah will come. In the light of Mary's song (Luke 1:55) and Zechariah's prophecy, we see how the expectations of the Messiah are rooted in the ancient promise.

*   *   *

It is always invigorating to be able to live with an eye to the future. Hope for the future lends flavor and zest to the present. We live in anticipation of things to come: the student cramming for final examinations anticipates the vacation period that will follow; the bridal couple have great hopes for their life together; the farmer planting his seed in the spring looks forward to a bumper crop in the fall; the young minister to a life of service; the clerk to his next promotion—and so it goes. Few of us are immune to the delights of expectation, even though it may refer to purely material things.

A different kind of expectancy was abroad in Israel at the time of Jesus' birth. Even then the precise details of the Messianic expectation were far from clear; yet Israel was unique among the nations in that the people had something to look forward to from the hand of God himself. We have seen it exemplified in Zechariah and Elizabeth "walking in all the commandments and ordinances of the Lord blameless." We meet it again in the aged Simeon, "righteous and devout, looking for the consolation of Israel" (2:25). We see it too in Anna, "worshiping with fasting and prayer night and day," and among those of her company "who were looking for the redemption of Jerusalem" (vv. 37f).

Obedience, righteousness, and worship point beyond themselves to a living hope—in this case, hope in God. Having nothing to look forward to is surely one of the great tragedies that can befall any person or people. It strips mankind of a reason for continuing to exist. Facing the future with nothing to hope for is a most desolate prospect indeed.

Christians share with the rest of humanity all the normal reasons for anticipating the future. Yet we ought not to be completely beguiled by these hopes. It frequently happens that the future, when it arrives, is much less pleasurable than we had anticipated; and sometimes it is not pleasurable at all. The student may fail his finals, and his holiday lie in ruins; the marriage may prove to be more than the young couple can sustain; the fall crop may return little more than the seed sown; the young minister, instead, may find that he has entered upon a life of tragedy; and the clerk's promotion may never come. The future realization of present hope is tenuous, tantalizing, and elusive—a circumstance which may have prompted Alexander Pope to write:

Hope springs eternal in the human breast:
Man never is, but always to be blest.

Is there, then, any *assured* hope? Anything of which fulfillment is beyond doubt? The Bible says there is. It is possible for Christians to live expectantly. Like Simeon and others, we have lived to see the fulfillment of the expectation of the people of God; much more, for they had seen only the baby, but we have seen the empty tomb. Christians can and do live in joyous expectancy; not by reason of those things which "moth and rust consume, and thieves break in and steal" (Matt. 6:19), but by the already fulfilled promise of our Lord that "he who believes in me, though he die, yet shall he live..." (John 11:25). Christians live in the knowledge that though "death may be our fate, God is our destiny" (McLelland). It is this assurance that gives identity, purpose, hope, zest, and joyous expectancy to our lives.

*   *   *

When Paul wrote to Timothy that "God our Savior... desires all men to be saved and to come to a knowledge of the truth" (1 Tim. 2:4), he was giving expression to God's age-long plan and purpose for all his creatures. The gospel is exclusively Jewish in origin, and world-wide in its fulfillment. It has been so since the inception of God's covenant with Abraham, a part of which reads: "... and in you all families of the earth will be blessed" (Revised Standard Version alternate reading). It was never God's purpose to save only Israelites, nor to confine his mercy to some, excluding others. Scripture is unanimous on that point. Accordingly, the good news announced by the angel at the birth of Jesus brought "great joy which will come to all people." Mary's inspired utterance in the Magnificat, "all generations will call me blessed," shows her appreciation of the magnitude and scope of God's work and purpose. Simeon, in his vision of "a light for revelation to the Gentiles," also knew it.

As the gospel was carried out into the world beyond Palestine and came in contact with the culture and religions of other peoples, Paul emerged as the most vigorous exponent of its universality. Peter had struck the same note in his preaching: "Truly I perceive that God shows no partiality, but in every nation anyone who fears him and does what is right is acceptable to him" (Acts 10:34). Paul went further: he eliminated national distinctions. "Here there cannot be Greek and Jew, circumcised and uncircumcised, barbarian, Scythian, slave, free man, but Christ is all, and in all" (Col. 3:11). And to the Galatians he wrote: "There is neither Jew nor Greek, there is neither slave nor free, there is neither male nor female; for you are all one in Christ" (3:28).

According to this teaching every person—man or woman—stands before God as the object of his mercy, grace, and redeeming love. His grace overcomes all those worldly distinctions normally accorded to each of us: race, color, privilege, wealth, station in life, sex, eminence, and intelligence. Salvation is offered to all, without restriction. And since "all have sinned and fall short of the glory of God" (Rom. 3:23), it is offered to sinners, too. There are no others.

In God's magnificent plan of salvation, proclaimed by the prophets and demonstrated in his Son Jesus Christ, he has accepted his errant people without reservation or exception. God's act of forgiveness has important implications for the church—for you and me. He has shown us the way; have we followed faithfully? Is our discipleship genuine or perfunctory? Are color, race, eminence, wealth, and social standing of no consequence to us, as they are to him? Or do the people of the world stand in the paradoxical position of being accepted by God and rejected by God's people? Surely the church's performance in this respect has not always and everywhere been completely satisfactory. Many of us have much to answer for.

*　　　　　*　　　　　*

Not many years ago there was a popular saying in Christian circles to the effect that "the youth of today are the church of tomorrow." Whether or not this particular gem of chronological wisdom is still current is not known; if it is, it has suffered some rude shocks in recent years. We may have to relearn, perhaps with some difficulty, that the church lives by the Spirit of God rather than by some process such as the passing of time.

This circumstance prompts the observation that in the Christmas story, as elsewhere in Scripture, prominence is given to some very senior citizens. In speaking of youth and age, especially in relation to the church, we ought not to play one against the other. There is no profit in that. Each has its own part to play and its own contribution to make to the enrichment of the life of God's people. David, for example, was a mere stripling when he killed the Philistine giant and delivered the Israelites from the hand of the enemy. Abraham was of advanced years when God summoned him from Ur. It is not age that is decisive in the service of God, but the call of God and the willingness to place one's talents and abilities at his disposal. The young may offer their vitality, enthusiasm, and ability to see things in a fresh light; the elderly may contribute their wisdom, experience, and sense of the continuity of God's people. If the "generation gap" has had unfortunate consequences in society, it has been a disaster in the church.

In addition to Abraham there are four elderly people whose names are mentioned in Luke's narrative of the birth of Jesus: Zechariah, Elizabeth, Simeon, and Anna. Considering the emphasis that Luke put on their advanced age, what particularly important contribution do they make to the story? And what can we learn from what we know of them? In each of them we see *patient* expectancy. Zechariah the priest and Elizabeth of priestly origin were not newcomers to the faith of Israel's God; Simeon had been promised that he would see the Lord's Christ during his lifetime; Anna had spent years in fasting and prayer, at no time forsaking the Temple. Patience of this kind is rare today. Our generation seems wedded to instant solutions and instant results. Some thoughtful people are suggesting that the natural impatience of youth is heightened in a generation accustomed to watching television programs in which serious problems seldom take more than sixty minutes to solve. Of course, impatience *in the faith* is not new, nor is it a characteristic peculiar to the young. "Wilt thou restrain thyself at these things, O Lord; wilt thou keep silent, and afflict us sorely?" (Isa. 64:12). The future of the church may rest with the young, but the strength of the church lies with those who "wait for the Lord" regardless of their age (Isa. 40:29–31). The equation representing endurance in the faith may be written as follows: hope + patience = strength. In this connection no age-group may lay claim to a monopoly.

FIVE

THE AFFIRMATION

Luke 1:80; 2:39-52 _____

THE DOCUMENTATION AVAILABLE TO US OF THE EARLY LIFE of John consists of a single verse of Scripture: "And the child grew and became strong in spirit, and he was in the wilderness till the day of his manifestation to Israel" (Luke 1:80). If we are looking for purely biographical material we are foredoomed to disappointment.

Accordingly, anything we say about John's early years must be tentative and provisional. We must be careful to say nothing that is not borne out by either the text or the sense of Scripture, and in keeping with our wider knowledge of his later life.

We are told that John grew "strong in spirit." We may assume, for one thing, that the years spent "in the wilderness" would have a profound effect on his character and personality. It would, perhaps, either "make or break" him. Moreover, the very word "wilderness" suggests a degree of isolation from society; this would involve isolation from the compromising influences that occur in one form or another in every community. Both of these observations—John's strength of character and purpose and his freedom from moral compromises—are consistent with what we know of him after "his manifestation to Israel."

The question remains as to why more attention is not given in Scripture to personal background information. We know more about John *before* his birth than we do of the years between his birth and the beginning of his ministry. We must conclude that although the human element is not entirely ignored, the vitally important thing is that John's life and ministry are God's work; which is to say, their origin was not in John's desert life but in the call of God. What was written of the prophet Jeremiah was true of John: "Before I formed you in the womb I knew you, and before you were born I consecrated you; I appointed you a prophet to the nations" (Jer. 1:5). Although John's life in the wilderness may have had some influence on the manner of his appearance, his actual message—repentance and forgiveness in the light of the coming of the Messiah—was of God.

The early life of Jesus was apparently more conventional. He was brought up in the small and inconspicuous village of Nazareth, surrounded by parents, brothers, and sisters. We have already seen something of Joseph's integrity and his readiness to heed God's unsupported word (Matt. 1:20), and of Mary's submission to God's will and purpose (Luke 1:38). There are two further references by which we are afforded an insight into the nature of the home in which Jesus was reared.

The first of these tells us that shortly after his birth, his parents, having "performed everything according to the law of the Lord," returned to Galilee (Luke 2:39). The second is the statement that they "went to Jerusalem every year at the feast of the Passover" (v. 41). There were probably thousands of Jewish parents of whom the same two statements might be made; yet Luke thinks it important for us to know that Jesus' parents were among them. Here again, however, a word of caution is needed. Luke is *not* trying to tell us that Jesus was mainly a product of his early environment. Had that been the author's intention he could surely have done a more persuasive job than he did. But Luke does seem to be observing that Joseph and Mary were faithful people—both to God and to their children. He was not prepared to discount the importance of early training of children. And if careful attention to such training was important within the holy family, it should not be a subject of indifference to us today.

The church believes and confesses that Jesus of Nazareth is in fact the Christ, the Son of God, and Savior of mankind. At a time of discouragement in adult years, John the Baptist sent his disciples to ask Jesus: "Are you he who is to come. . . ?" (Matt. 11:3; Luke 7:19; read Matt. 11:2–6; Luke 7:18–23). We who are Christians have no doubt that John's question must be answered in the affirmative. This is our faith, largely because we are able to "read the Gospels backward"—as it were, from Easter to Christmas. It is in and by the resurrection that Jesus' identity, as the Son of God who comes as the Messiah, is fully disclosed. It is because we believe this that we study his life and ministry, and ponder his every word.

Coming to the study of Scripture, as most of us do, from a family tradition of Christian faith, we do so with an almost implicit assumption that Jesus is the promised Savior; and thus we read the Scriptures in that light. But we do not get very far along in these studies before realizing that Jesus himself seldom if ever made the explicit claim that he was the Messiah. Some of his utterances were puzzling for that very reason. In the example referred to above, he did not answer John's question with a direct "yes" or "no," but pointed to what he was doing then and told his questioners to go and report to John what they had seen. The passages cited above from Matthew and Luke describe this eloquently. He also took great care on some occasions to see that his Messiahship was not openly declared. This, as we noted previously, is one of the most prominent features of Mark's Gospel.

This raises the question of Jesus' own awareness of his identity. At what point in his life did Jesus become convinced that he was the promised deliverer and that God's promise to Abraham was fulfilled in him? This is what we call the "Messianic consciousness" of Jesus. Did he have this from birth? While conversing with the teachers in the Temple? At the time of his baptism? Or at some other period during the course of his ministry?

Although it is natural for us to speculate on this matter, we must note that the New Testament does not encourage us to do so; nor does it offer us much material on which to base our speculation. An outstanding German scholar, Günther Bornkamm, has written in his book *Jesus of Nazareth*: "We should however remember that what mattered most for the Gospels and the tradition was the fact that Jesus *was* the Messiah. . . ." He points out that the question of our Lord's "consciousness" is modern and somewhat psychological; and that on this question, conceived in this way, the Gospels "remain extremely indifferent." Bornkamm further comments that Jesus does not first of all proclaim "his own rank as a special theme of his message." Rather, "Jesus is to be found *in* his word and *in* his actions." In other words, Jesus presents himself and asks for a decision of faith on what people see in his words and deeds, as with John the Baptist in the incident referred to above.

In the passage of Scripture before us Jesus answered his mother's query with the words: "Did you not know that I must be in my Father's house?" (v. 49). The particular phrase, "my Father's house," could in a general sense be used by any devout person. In Luke it doubtless is meant to imply something more. Although, as has been said, the Gospels do not deal with the question of Jesus' "consciousness" in the way that a modern biographer might, the Gospel writers reflected faith in Jesus as the Messiah. We may therefore assume that these words are not offhand or casual. As Christians looking back from the resurrection, we can see how they carried the sense of a unique relationship to God—God, the Father of our Lord Jesus Christ.

The whole passage serves as a link between the birth of Jesus and his adult ministry in Luke's Gospel. But it does more than this. As to its deeper meaning, the Gospel includes it not so much to indicate what Jesus thought about himself, as to show him speaking with authority even as a child; and speaking on the basis of a profound understanding of the Old Testament Scriptures. The account is not given to portray a "child prodigy," as is often the case with stories told about great men (and was true of some of the stories that were later developed about Jesus outside the New Testament). If this narrative were taken alone, without knowledge of the gospel as a whole, we might be puzzled by it; and in fact we would be presumptuous to claim that we clearly understand everything in this account as written.

Yet Jesus is certainly acting as God's Son, and the Christian can hardly fail to see this as the primary meaning and importance of the passage in Luke's Gospel. Also to be observed is that Jesus, absorbed in matters of his Father's house, actually rebukes Mary and Joseph (v. 49). There is friction already between the demands of the natural home and the ultimate demands that Jesus' divine Sonship will make. This conflict, now anticipated in this very restrained story, will become painful in adult years. But it is also significant that Jesus in these early years follows the pattern of obedience by coming home to Nazareth, and *obeying* those with authority over him as a child (v. 50).

The vital importance of the early training of children can

scarcely be exaggerated; and this statement can be documented from almost every home, school, and church in the nation. Training for what? In this case, training in preparation: for making wise decisions, for acceptance by God, and for receiving the respect and esteem of fellow-members of society.

It is probably true that no two children can be brought up and trained in exactly the same way; and if this is so, there is no universally applicable formula for doing so. Nevertheless, this is no sufficient reason for parents to abdicate their responsibilities in this respect. Every parent is answerable to God for the proper care of his or her child. The subjects of child training and youth guidance are so wide-ranging and well-nigh inexhaustible that we will be content to make a few brief observations as to how these affect the church.

(a) Parents who say, "We do not go to church ourselves but we see that the children get to Sunday School" are frauds. They are fooling themselves and trying, unsuccessfully, to deceive God (and probably the minister).

(b) Parents who do not pray with and for their children are demonstrating their conviction that they can "go it alone." If the time should come when they find they can't, they are frequently among the first to ask, "Why did this happen to me?"

(c) Many parents refuse to "force" their children to sit through a service of public worship on the grounds that the young folk don't understand it. This has a certain plausibility—until we ask, "How else are they going to find out?" (read Deut. 6). This chapter understands the situation perfectly, and we would do well to listen. Learning by rote, although at variance with current theories of secular education, nevertheless has a long and honorable history when used intelligently.

*   *   *

It is striking that the Gospels provide so little information about Jesus' life between the ages of twelve and approximately thirty. Some scholars look upon this void with considerable regret. The absence of biographical detail pertaining to this period has prompted students of the New Testament to call these the "hidden years."

The Christian Church has always maintained that Jesus was both uniquely the Son of God and fully human. On that basis some Christian educators have felt free to speak of experiences that Jesus *may* have had, of such a nature as to enrich his parables and other teachings. In their zeal to give the person of our Lord a kind of reality, and perhaps intending to lend support to his genuine humanity, some religious education courses even tell "stories of Jesus" which have no foundation in Scripture at all.

It is natural to suppose that Jesus did enjoy the normal experiences of adolescence and young manhood in accordance with the customs of the day. He would probably have walked in the fields of grain with his friends, picked fruit, admired flowers, attended synagogue, and gone to school. Yet it is difficult to understand what useful purpose is served by inventing stories to fill the gap; and it may be very dangerous to do so. The reality of Jesus' humanity is thereby made to rest on fictional material. Evidence of the humanity of Jesus, however, is to be found in his human birth—"born of a woman," as Paul says—to which the Gospels attest. The danger in believing fictional stories of his youth is simply that they evaporate with maturity, leaving only uncertainty or unbelief.

Perhaps we should accept and even embrace the silence of the hidden years, rather than try to fill them with the fruit of reverent conjecture. Paul appears to have sensed the difference when, in writing to the Corinthian church, he declared: "From now on, therefore, we regard no one from a human point of view; even though we once regarded Christ from a human point of view, we regard him thus no longer" (2 Cor. 5:16).

SIX

THE ACCEPTANCE

Mark 1:4–13 _____ Luke 3:1–22; 4:1–3

MARK WRITES LIKE A MAN IN A HURRY TO GET TO THE POINT,
and his abruptness is often refreshing. No genealogy, no birth
story, no account of the incident in the Temple as in Matthew
and Luke, and no theologizing as is found in the first chapter of
John. We have a single verse which might serve as a title, a
connecting link with the Old Testament, mention of the
forerunner—with these swift, deft strokes the story begins. We
owe, of course, a tremendous debt to the other evangelists for
details which Mark does not provide. Yet Mark's writing has a
directness and an urgency about it that is at once delightful and
profound. The sequence in the brief statements of Mark 1:9–13
suggests that Jesus was learning, as it were, what he was up
against; weighing the forces which would be exerted against his
ministry, and facing the future, whatever it might bring.

The dawn of the new—that is, the Messianic—age is presented in the Gospels as the moment of climax in human history.
It is at once the fulfillment of the promise made by God to
Abraham, the historical realization of two thousand years of Hebrew prophecy, and the visible verification of the faithfulness of
Israel's God. John, the last of the prophets, "prepares the way"
by preaching baptism for the remission of sins, and by calling for
an ethical life-style consistent with genuine repentance. Jesus
offers himself as a candidate for John's baptism; John demurs,
saying that _he_ needs to be baptized by Jesus (Matt. ch. 3). Jesus
pursues the matter, saying that they should "fulfill all righteousness," and is baptized.

It is not difficult to believe that Jesus' reply to John's question

–31–

was originally intended to withhold, rather than to reveal, his reason for desiring baptism. Certainly Jesus—the sinless one— had no sins to be remitted and no need to repent. Nevertheless, John was calling all Israel to repent and be baptized, and it had pleased God that his Son should be born an Israelite. It was then as an Israelite—according to his humanity—that Jesus insisted on being baptized by John. In this way he did two things: he confirmed the (temporary) validity of John's baptism, and he declared his own solidarity with Israel—and, looking to the future, with all God's people at all times and in all places. Jesus, that is to say, is one of us.

It is possible too that at this stage of his life, while yet facing and appraising his future before beginning his ministry, Jesus did not wish to make an exception of himself. Considering the overwhelming response to John's call, Jesus would surely have made himself conspicuous by opting out of John's baptism. It may have been this kind of attention that Jesus did not want at this time.

Baptism is regarded in the church as an ordinance (sacrament) symbolic of death and resurrection: going down into the water as into death, and coming to the surface as to newness of life. It demonstrates the symbolic portrayal of dying and rising again. That most Reformed Churches have practiced sprinkling rather than immersion does not change the significance of the act (though it may have made it less explicit). It is apparent that in the thinking of both Jesus (Luke 12:50; Mark 10:39) and Paul (Rom. 6:3), baptism and death were closely linked. Jesus evidently foresaw his own death as a kind of baptism, and by referring to it preserved the symbolism and indirectly foretold his own resurrection. Thus Jesus, in accepting baptism at the hands of John, was consciously taking the first irrevocable step that would lead inexorably to his death so that, as Paul teaches, by his resurrection "we too might walk in newness of life" (Rom. 6:4). If this is so, the implications of Jesus' baptism for our conduct are the same as those of his death, since we are "baptized into his death." They cannot be described more clearly than Paul has done in the same chapter (viz. 6:12–14).

It may be useful to think for a moment of Jesus at this point sizing up the situation, or in the language of the Bible, "counting the cost." We cannot doubt that our Lord was by this time thoroughly aware of his identity as uniquely the Son of God, particularly in the light of the declaration by the Holy Spirit at his baptism. He was to be the deliverer, the Savior of his people. He would perhaps try to assess the strength of the powers ranged against him, and to set a course for the accomplishment of his mission.

It is important to observe that the same Holy Spirit who had attested Jesus' Sonship also "drove him out into the wilderness." There he encountered the adversary—the very spirit of evil, the strange, malignant presence that is embedded in all of human life and pervades all its aspects. It can be said that this confrontation with the devil was so traumatic an experience for our Lord that at no time in his subsequent ministry did he lose sight of his enemy for a single moment. He was not drawn away into side issues nor distracted by lesser problems.

The three temptations of Jesus have been variously described and interpreted by many different scholars. The first, as related by Matthew, may be considered as an appeal to Jesus to demonstrate his power over the elements as evidence of his Sonship. Why would he not change stones into bread when not long afterward he changed water into wine? The circumstances of the two incidents were, of course, entirely different. There was no need for Jesus to prove his identity in the presence of the devil; the devil knew perfectly well with whom he was dealing. The Gospels give abundant evidence that evil spirits knew who Jesus was, often long before the people did. Jesus would not use his power flippantly. The miracle (sign) in Cana, on the other hand, was performed in company and before witnesses, as a result of which "his disciples believed in him."

The second temptation (again following Matthew) was probably the most impertinent: an invitation to Jesus to place himself in jeopardy deliberately in order to test the validity of God's word. Jesus, knowing very well that God would be there when he needed him, would not yield. Faith, as the need may arise, is daring but never foolhardy. The second temptation was, perhaps, the most insulting.

Nothing pleases evil quite as much as having good as its servant; and nothing would have pleased the devil more than to know that the Son of God was his devotee. The third temptation was just that: that Jesus should worship the devil, deriving strength from evil. (There is literally nothing the devil won't try!) Jesus' reply shows plainly that in this conflict there is no place for divided or shared loyalties: "You shall worship the Lord your God, and him only shall you serve."

Jesus' temptations, diverse as they were in substance and scenery, were nevertheless all of a piece. At the beginning of his ministry Jesus was being asked to accept another lord than God, to forsake the leading, guidance, and partnership of God's Holy Spirit, and to use other means to accomplish his mission than sole dependence on the word and will of the heavenly Father. Having just accepted baptism, having been visited by the Holy Spirit (who had not left him), and having been acknowledged by God as "my beloved Son with whom I am well pleased," Jesus is now being asked whether there is any possibility of compromise. The answer is "no." If there was no possibility of compromise for Jesus, it follows as day follows night that compromise is not a live option for you and me.

It has often been said that the Bible can be used to support either side of almost any argument. A conspicuous example, coming readily to mind, is capital punishment. Scripture, however, should not necessarily be abandoned as inherently self-contradictory, and so without binding authority. The true alternative is to embrace Scripture more firmly, study it more closely, and understand it more fully.

A number of small but important lessons are to be learned from Jesus' encounter with the devil. One is that Scripture is not likely to be very convincing to one who does not believe or trust in God. Second, we may learn from the devil that mere familiarity with Scripture is no substitute for understanding it. Third, we may learn from Jesus that if we do not know what Scripture says, we *cannot* know what it means.

As mentioned in the previous chapter, modern theories of secular education seem largely to have dispensed with the method of learning by rote. That this decision has any bearing on education in the church is not clear. The picture, so dear to the hearts of modern educators, of hordes of disgruntled children slavishly committing reams of Scripture to memory, is an unnecessary and unfaithful caricature of reality. In any event, when Jesus was faced with temptation he did not have to run home for a copy of the Old Testament to defend himself. It was, so to speak, at his fingertips; and, as a result, he survived this supreme test of strength and conviction. Thoroughly grounded as he was in the Scriptures and traditions of his people, he was able to draw on them freely for his defense.

Surely in considering the equipment necessary for the Christian's defense against evil—to which Paul has referred as "the whole armor of God" (Ephes. 6:11–17)—a primary place must be given to a thorough knowledge of God's written word. We have seen that it was of immense importance to Jesus; it can scarcely be less so to us.

On the whole, the Spirit of God is mentioned much less frequently in the first three Gospels than might be expected. He was present at the incarnation (Matt. 1:18, 20), to Elizabeth (Luke 1:41), to Zechariah (1:67), to Simeon (2:26), at Jesus' baptism, in the wilderness, and upon Jesus' return to Galilee. In the synagogue at Nazareth, where Jesus began his ministry, he read: "The Spirit of God is upon me . . . ," and all further direct reference to the person of the Spirit is withheld. We must go to the fourth Gospel and to the writings of St. Paul for fuller discussion of the work of the Spirit in the human heart and in the life of the church. Yet we cannot seriously doubt that God's Holy Spirit was our Lord's constant companion throughout the remainder of his life.

A curious and interesting pair of alternative readings of Luke 4:1 is provided by the K.J.V. ("Jesus . . . was led by the Spirit into the wilderness") and the R.S.V. ("Jesus . . . was led by the Spirit . . . in the wilderness"). In the newer translation the entire meaning has been altered. In one, Jesus' entry into the wilderness was instigated by the Spirit. In the other is the simple statement that while Jesus was in the wilderness he received the guidance of the Spirit. Matthew's testimony (4:1) is stronger than either of the other two, and favors the meaning conveyed by the K.J.V. of Luke: "Jesus was led up by the Spirit into the wilderness (in order?) to be tempted by the devil." On this reading, the Spirit's decision to expose Jesus to temptation appears deliberate. If this is correct, it is doubly comforting because it shows the Spirit of God in complete command. Jesus must face his arch-enemy at some point in his ministry; he must be confronted by "the wiles of the devil" sooner or later; and he must have first-hand experience of the power and subtlety of evil. And because he did so, "he is able to help those who are tempted" (Heb. 2:18b). All this the Spirit "arranged."

In seeking to understand the importance of the Spirit in the life of Jesus, we are affirming his humanity. The temptations were real enough; desperately real. Yet such was the power of the Spirit attending him that our Lord was able to endure the test without sin (Heb. 4:15).

In the story of the temptations of Jesus there stands revealed the fundamental nature of his mission—to overthrow and conquer the enormous, malevolent power of evil that holds the world in thrall. Jesus' task is therefore not concerned merely with problems of human conduct, to teach us what is right as opposed to what is wrong, or to provide us with a wholesome example. The conflict takes place at the deeper level of good and evil, obedience and disobedience. It has to do with what our forefathers called "mysterium iniquitatis"—the mystery of evil as it pervades a fallen world. To regard Jesus of Nazareth as primarily a teacher of moral precepts is faint praise indeed for him who partook of our nature, "that he through death might destroy him who has the power of death, that is, the devil..." (Heb. ch. 2). The conflict in the wilderness was inconclusive. Jesus did not yield; the devil withdrew but did not give up. It was not until later, at Calvary and at Joseph's tomb, that the devil learned who is in charge; for it was in subjecting himself to the power of sin, death, and the devil, and by his triumphant resurrection from the grave that Jesus put the devil to flight.

For you and me this is an unequal contest. "Your adversary the devil prowls around like a roaring lion, seeking someone to devour" (1 Peter 5). Let us not think that alone and unaided we can make our way safely. The devil has lost the power of death, but not the subtlety to deceive. In his hands, without God's word and Spirit, you and I are helpless.

SEVEN

THE DECLARATION

Mark 1:14–15 _____ Luke 4:14–30

WHEN JESUS RETURNED TO GALILEE AFTER THE TEMPTATIONS
in the wilderness, a "report" concerning him was circulating in
the surrounding country. We have no means of knowing the
substance of that report. Perhaps it concerned the unusual circumstances which attended his baptism. In any case, Jesus was
being talked about, and it was not entirely fanciful to suggest that
he had become a kind of local celebrity. In that capacity, he began
at first to teach in the synagogues of the region. Then as now, the
truly gifted teacher was easily recognized, and the people were
not slow to honor him—Luke says that he was "glorified by all"
(Luke 4:15).

Jesus did not, however, absent himself from regular synagogue worship, as we see from v. 16. Although he preached in
the countryside and the villages, he did not live or minister without regard to the traditional places where his people gathered for
worship and instruction. This can be seen from the description of
his visit to the synagogue in Nazareth. His opportunity to read
came doubtless at the invitation of the president of the synagogue,
issued a few days before the sabbath (vv. 16f).

The expectations of the people concerning the Messiah were
running high. What kind of king or military leader would he be?
How would he assert his ascendancy and maintain his rule? And
how would he get rid of those domineering Roman soldiers who
were garrisoned throughout the land?

When Jesus chose a synagogue in which to announce his
Messiahship and the nature of his mission, he set himself apart
from all secular aspirants to political power and military prowess.

The words he read (from Isa. 61:1f) declared the loving-kindness of the Lord. There is a subdued note in Luke's narrative as he tells of Jesus reading, closing the book, returning it to the attendant and being seated—perhaps in deliberate contrast to the fanfare that one might expect on so momentous an occasion. It is apparent from the words with which Jesus chose to introduce his ministry that he had chosen to follow God's way rather than a purely human way of "leadership." He would be servant-king, not oriental despot. He would serve the true interests of his people, rather than the dictates of his personal ego. If there was to be violence in the Kingdom it would be theirs, not his.

Jesus' entire ministry and "rule" corresponded to another phrase from the same prophet: "For my thoughts are not your thoughts, neither are your ways my ways, says the Lord. For as the heavens are higher than the earth, so are my ways higher than your ways, and my thoughts than your thoughts" (Isa. 55:8f). It would be interesting and intensely profitable to study the four Gospels with this one thing in mind: to note the occasions in the ministry of Jesus in which values commonly accepted by society in his world and ours are authoritatively reversed by him.

It has often been remarked that the structure of modern society, almost of necessity, tends to depersonalize the individual. In many of our contacts, if we have not actually become *things*, we are nevertheless regarded as groups, classes, and even numbers. The doctor deals with people but speaks of them as "cases"; the social worker has a "clientele" and a "case-load"; a minister has "members" of a congregation. To the telephone company and the bank, to social security and welfare offices, to the license bureau and Medicare, to the postman and the credit agencies, we are little more than numbers. Because it belittles our dignity as human beings we resent being thought of in this way. Little wonder, then, that TV advertising so consistently emphasizes the personal concern of this or that huge industrial conglomerate for the individual consumer, however unreal that concern may in fact be.

Truth to tell, it is difficult to see how it could be otherwise, given the rapid technological change, the immense influx of people to urban areas, and the increasing complexity of life today. Yet the personal element must surely be preserved or recaptured. Our Lord's commandment to love our neighbor makes it imperative for us to see him or her as more than an abstraction. For purposes of convenience, and to grasp the nature and size of human problems, people in some way need to be "classified." Thus there are poor, there are captives, there are some who are oppressed. Yet in actual life one does not deal with a class but with an individual, with a person. It has often been said, and rightly, that the poor need people at least as much as they need money.

The words Jesus chose from Isaiah to inaugurate his ministry show clearly that he did not have mere humanitarianism in mind. He preached "good news"—an expression previously used by John the Baptist (Luke 3:18) when announcing the imminence of the kingdom of God and the coming of the Messiah. Jesus also proclaimed the "acceptable year of the Lord," i.e. the year of the Lord's favor. The good works of Jesus were a sign that the day of the Lord was at hand.

It was doubtless an exhilarating experience for those gathered in the synagogue at Nazareth to hear their own scriptures read by one of their own young men. His further statement, that the prophecy he had just read had also been fulfilled, made the occasion complete. Now the blessings of the Messianic age were "just around the corner." The people, to put it mildly, were pleased, and "all spoke well of him" (v. 22).

In the light of what followed, we might surmise that this incident at Nazareth later prompted Jesus to warn the multitude—the disciples being within easy ear-shot—"Woe unto you when all men speak well of you, for so their fathers did to the false prophets" (6:26). (The situations were not identical, but they were analogous.) "Their fathers" (ancestors) welcomed the words of the *false* prophets, believing them to be true because they were congenial. Jesus' contemporaries rejoiced at his (true) words because they misunderstood them. When they did understand them correctly, the people resorted to violence, as we see in ch. 4:28-30.

Yet in spite of their eager acceptance of Jesus' words, the people began to doubt, to raise questions. The implications were, on second thought, startling. It was inconceivable that "Joseph's son," whom all these people knew, could be the Messiah, God's anointed servant. Accordingly, Jesus anticipated what they would next want to ask—namely, will you give us a sign in proof of your claim? At the same time he showed his sympathetic appreciation of their difficulty, recognizing that the prophet is rarely accepted by his own people (vv. 23f). We might have said it differently: "Familiarity breeds contempt," which comes to us from one of Aesop's fables. Their genuine familiarity, for a span of thirty years, with Jesus' human attributes stood in the way of their ready acceptance of his divinity.

Instead of satisfying their unspoken desire for proof, Jesus used the occasion to broaden their religious horizons—doubtless knowing how much offense he would give (vv. 25ff). The God whom they worshiped was certainly Israel's God; but he was not and never had been the God of Israel alone. Of this Jesus gave two illustrations from their own literature which showed God's grace to those of other nations: the story of the Syro-Phoenician woman of Zarephath in Sidon, to whom God ministered because she trusted the bare word of the prophet Elijah; and Naaman the Syrian, who was healed of leprosy because he believed in the unsupported word of Elisha (see 1 Kings 17:8-24; 2 Kings 5:1-14). By these illustrations our Lord appears to have been saying two things: (1) that God's love and concern had never been confined solely to Israel; and (2) that like Naaman and the widow of Zarephath his hearers should believe the word now, and they would see miracles later.

Religious unbelief (and conviction) can prompt people to do the most vicious things. On this occasion, what began as a most congenial gathering ended in violence. To have their supposed place as God's favorites thus challenged was more than the congregation in Nazareth could tolerate. So monstrous was their rage that they tried to kill Jesus then and there.

What enraged the people at Nazareth recurred often in Jesus' teaching. We may recall, as one example, how Jesus told the story of the Great Supper (Luke 14:16-24) as a warning to those for whom it was prepared that, should they ignore the invitation, their places would be taken by others. That parable closes with the master's words: "None of those men who were invited shall taste of my banquet."

This theme is further substantiated in the ministry of Paul and Barnabas. Over against some Jewish Christians who insisted that Gentiles must first become members of Judaism if they were to become members of the church, Paul maintained a firm stand. Knowing that Christ's grace was for everyone, both by word and action he sought to bring all persons together within the kingdom of God—made one by Israel's Messiah.

Is there not something we can learn today from these illustrations? We believe that God has not changed, that he wills that there be a people called in his name. We believe that we have this calling, that we are in fact "the new Israel." As such, we have entered into the promises of the Israel of old. But does this fact separate us from the world? Are we to imagine that we can stand apart from what God asks of his people in their work and witness upon earth? Are we so isolated and self-contained that we can be indifferent to the troubles and the corruptions of private and public life? Can we look at all that is wrong and assert our innocence, as though it had nothing to do with the church? Is our faith to be kept within our own group, for our enjoyment and not in service to all people? And, to reverse the situation at Nazareth, do we suppose that God has accepted us and excluded the Jews from the ultimate fulfillment of his promises to them?

It is often said that western Christendom, including the North American continent, is for all practical purposes one huge mission field. Black and brown and yellow Christians now come to us from the Third World to tell of the triumphs of the gospel in their countries. Is the gospel passing once again from the hands of those to whom it earlier came? And if so, is it because of our unfaithfulness?

*   *   *

The significance and importance of baptism as a rite and/or sacrament of the church have been explained and expounded for two thousand years. According to some Books of Common Order, it is a "sign and seal of the washing away of our sin and our ingrafting into Christ." It is symbolic of death and resurrection as taught by the apostle Paul. It is a sign of regeneration, and the rite of initiation into membership in the church.

Let us consider the possibility that for Jesus the acceptance of baptism was itself a declaration of purpose. At the time of his baptism Jesus was a grown man—some thirty years of age. His request for baptism was therefore a mature decision. From the way in which his request was defended (when John objected), we learn that it was in some way an act of obedience. For Jesus, baptism seems to have been a way of stating his purpose, a clear indication of his intention to pursue a life of obedience to the Father, and of service to all mankind.

Perhaps that is an aspect of what baptism should mean to us as well. If so, then the practice of infant baptism tends to obscure it. But having been baptized, many of us in infancy, we can no longer postpone a serious consideration of those obligations which were laid upon us by this act.

Since none of the evangelists who tell the story of the temptations mentions a companion, we are probably correct in assuming that Jesus was alone with the Spirit of God and the power of the devil. Jesus faced the alternatives alone; the decision was his. No coterie of friends was by his side, no parents, well-wishers, or counsellors. He was under no pressure; he had no one to please.

How different it so frequently is in the modern church! It may be that a minister believes that young people should "join" the church at a particular age, and makes a special effort to enlist his teen-agers as members of the congregation. There are parents who believe that children have a duty to declare their faith at an appropriate time. A husband may unite with the church to please his wife or a wife at the urging of her husband.

This is all very well; it is good to have support in making so momentous a commitment—and happy are they who have it. But a decision to join the church *for these reasons* is open to serious question. The decision is and must be a personal decision, arrived at simply because one believes deeply in Jesus Christ as Son of God and Savior of mankind. When that conviction is lacking, one enters neither the church of Jesus Christ nor the kingdom of God.

EIGHT
THE ENLISTMENT

Mark 1:16–20; 3:13–19 _____ Luke 5:1–11; 6:12–16; 9:1–6

EACH OF THE FOUR EVANGELISTS INCLUDES IN HIS GOSPEL
an account of the calling of the disciples. As the Old Israel was a
twelve-fold body of tribes, the New Israel was conceived in like
manner, with twelve leaders. One might like to record that Jesus
selected his associates with meticulous care and unerring insight;
and that as a result all twelve were strong, faithful, and true. As
we know, this did not seem to be the case. We have no means of
knowing by what criteria our Lord chose the men he did. We do
know, however, that these twelve, as a body, did not provide the
effective leadership of the church after the Lord's death. Certain
of them became recognized leaders of the primitive Christian
community—notably Peter. But others seem to have played little
part; and the leadership passed to men like Paul and James the
Lord's brother, who did not belong to the original twelve. By
Mark's time very little was known of them or of the parts they
played. In any event, it seems clear that the twelve disciples
formed a cross-section of those who believed rather than a carefully selected elite.

The foregoing paragraph does not suggest that Jesus' choice of
disciples was thoughtless or haphazard. He doubtless gave a great
deal of thought to those whom he would choose. Luke tells us
that the night before the disciples were called was spent in prayer.
It is reasonable to suppose that our Lord asked for wisdom in the
selections he was about to make; it could hardly be otherwise.
Most scholars have made this observation. There is an additional
possibility: that Jesus' extended prayer was a prayer *for* the disciples he was about to choose. No one knew as he did the rigors of

discipleship and the hardships of obedience. None could foresee the difficulties they would encounter and the sacrifices they would be called upon to make. Unlike Jesus himself, none whom he would choose had so far been tested by the devil, and none knew his power. The disciples would come with him much as Abraham went with God: "not knowing where (they) were to go" (Heb. 11:8). So, we believe, Jesus prayed for them, interceding with God on their behalf. Regardless of whom Jesus might choose to be his disciples, his choice would fall on mortal men— with all the frailties that are our common lot. He who "always lives to make intercession for those who draw near to God through him" (Heb. 7:25) must surely have offered prayer beforehand for those whom he would soon call to be his disciples.

As a first order of business, so to speak, Jesus gathered about him a group of persons who would share with him the work of his mission. As we know from experience, the call to become a Christian is issued individually and responded to personally. Yet in the nature of the call the disciples, in making a decision, thereby became members of a group. A Christian in isolation from all other Christians is very nearly a contradiction in terms.

Except for the similarity of the number of tribes of Israel to the number of disciples originally chosen, we do not know why our Lord limited the number of the group to twelve (Rev. 21:12–14; Acts 1:15–26). Would six or eight have been less effective? Would sixteen or twenty have been unwieldy? Again, we do not know. In any event we may be assured that Jesus did not single out these men merely for companionship, but for active duty—participation. Being a disciple is therefore not the same thing as being a patron; discipleship is honorable, of course, but not honorary. The disciple enlists for service, not status—as so many seem to do today.

Jesus appointed the twelve "to be with him" and "to be sent out to preach." As we shall see, these men were both given authority and subject to authority. They were not "free-lance" evangelists. Their having been with him was a necessary prerequisite of their going out to preach. Jesus not only gave them their commissions; he interpreted their experiences to them and comforted them in their inevitable failures. Only so could the unity of the group be preserved.

Jesus seems to have had at least three reasons for appointing disciples to accompany him and work with him. Although exact dates are difficult to establish, we feel reasonably certain that Jesus' ministry did not last longer than three years, and may have been as brief as a year and a half. Our Lord might well have felt the need to publicize his work as widely as possible in the short time at his disposal. In this respect the situation was not unlike that of Moses (Exod. 18), who had more to do than one man could be expected to accomplish alone, and appointed judges to assist him in caring for the people. Jesus undoubtedly wished to share his mission with others, to allow others to participate with him in the proclamation of the kingdom. Paul once called the church "fellow workmen for God" (1 Cor. 3:9); the disciples were fellow workmen for Jesus. They could not inaugurate the kingdom; that had already been done in the appearance of Jesus, the Messiah. They could, however, proclaim it far and wide, and make trial of its powers. Finally, discipleship during Jesus' lifetime was a preparation and an apprenticeship for their work in later years when Jesus would no longer be among them. No finer training could be imagined.

*　　　　*　　　　*

It is of course pointless to assign responsibility and then withhold authority. The two are mutually complementary. Luke (9:1f) is explicit in saying that Jesus both commissioned the disciples and empowered them. These words, we may be sure, were written for our sakes so that we may understand the situation and the mandate clearly. As a first point, in the prosecution of their assignment the disciples are not completely on their own. Neither the proclamation of the kingdom nor the healing of the sick will depend on their gifts, talents, or strength. The power is not inherent in them; it is Jesus' gift to be used for one purpose only—and certainly not for self-aggrandizement. Again, there is a striking likeness to an incident in Moses' leadership of Israel. When Moses complained that he could not satisfy the needs of the people, he was instructed to seek out seventy men "whom you know to be elders of the people . . . and I will take some of the spirit which is upon you and put it on them . . ." (Num. 11:16f).

It is in like manner that we modern disciples are to understand our calling. Such power and authority as has been given to us ought not to be seen otherwise than as gifts of God for the pursuance of the assignment originating in Jesus and continued by the early disciples. But without that gift of power they, and we, are equally helpless.

Our helplessness in proclaiming the kingdom and healing men's ills is ingeniously illustrated in connection with Jesus' promise that his disciples would "henceforth be catching men" (Luke 5:10). In that episode our Lord had commanded Peter to "let down the nets for a catch." Peter protested, yet consented. "Master we have toiled all night and took nothing. But *at your word* I will let down the nets." The rest is history; and that history confirms that the criterion of true and fruitful discipleship is obedience to Jesus' words.

The obligation to be loyal, faithful, and committed has not changed materially with the passing of the years since Jesus' time on earth. But the world has; it is constantly undergoing change—in some periods more rapidly than in others. Accordingly, the circumstances and context of our commitment will not be precisely the same as they were even forty years ago. In many ways it is more difficult to be a truly faithful servant of the gospel now than it was then. Among the reasons for this we may note the following: two World Wars fought in part between nations having virtually identical Christian traditions, with the paradoxical consequence of prayers arising to the same God from both warring camps; an expanded and popularized study of historic religions, leading many people to believe that Christian faith is just one of many; the recent scientific (including medical) advances leading to a resurgence of pride in human achievement and the worship of secular gods; the increasingly pervasive influence of a strongly hedonistic interpretation of life; and the constantly increasing mobility of the population, which puts enormous strain on the stability of family units.

These are some of the factors which make faithful Christian service exceedingly difficult today. One might say that the "opposition" to faith is stronger, and that the difficulties are more numerous than in almost any previous age. Accordingly, a greater measure of responsibility accrues to Christian people for their individual witness, and to the church for the vitality of its corporate presence. There is a very great need today for genuine allegiance and total commitment, and therefore for exemplary rather than nominal Christians. Paul said it admirably in his letter to the Philippians (2:1-4) as translated by J. B. Phillips:

> Now if your experience of Christ's encouragement and love mean anything to you, if you have known something of the fellowship of his Spirit, and all that it means in kindness and deep sympathy, do make my best hopes for you come true! Live together in harmony, live together in love, as though you had only one mind and one spirit between you. Never act from motives of rivalry or personal vanity, but in humility think more of each other than you do of yourselves. None of you should think only of his own affairs, but should learn to see things from other people's point of view.

It is truly surprising to realize how little assured knowledge of the disciples is afforded us in the New Testament. Matthew had been a tax-gatherer (publican); James and John, those "sons of thunder," were fishermen; Simon Peter, Andrew's brother, was a bit more self-confident than situations sometimes warranted; Thomas seems to have been hard to convince; and Judas may have had a tendency to ask, "What's in it for me?" None of the lists of the disciples gives us much more than a name, an occupation, and/or a relationship. Perhaps the one thing we can be sure of about the Twelve is that they were a diverse group; as we have said, a cross-section of those who believed.

This is not as unimportant as we might suppose. It suggests, first of all, that one does not have to conform to any one pattern in order to be a Christian. It matters not whether one works manually or intellectually, whether self-employed or government official, prosperous or financially insecure, a person of letters or of little education. Indeed, a good many things do not matter in being a Christian. Happily, we find the same traits exhibited in the church today. Its membership is drawn from a fairly representative cross-section of the population (weighted a bit heavily, perhaps, by the predominant middle and upper middle classes).

It was Paul, rather than the Gospel writers, who first drew

attention to the significance and value of diversity in the church. (Paul's letters are generally believed to have preceded in time the work of the Gospel writers.) His treatment of the subject in the first Corinthian letter (ch. 12) is magnificent. There he enumerates the wealth and variety of the gifts of God to his church, recognizing each as indispensable to the completeness of the whole, and showing that none is more or less important than the others. The gifts thus enumerated are seen to be "manifestations of the Spirit," to be used "for the common good." The author of these diverse gifts is God the Holy Spirit. The apportionment of them is not always uniform: "he apportions to each one individually as he wills." (In the Old Testament we have the "major" and the "minor" prophets. The same situation prevails in the church today.) But the gifts given to each are essential to the whole.

In a related passage (Ephes. 4:12ff), Paul speaks more briefly of the gifts and at greater length of their purpose: "for the equipment of the saints for the work of the ministry, for building up the body of Christ . . . ." (Note: we dispense with the comma after the word "saints" for the reason that apostles, prophets, etc. are already exercising a ministry, and that they are doing so for the purpose of equipping other believers for a ministry of their own. Every believer has a ministry to exercise.) The intent in both passages is the same, though expressed differently. "For the common good" may be understood as "building up the body of Christ" in membership and depth of conviction.

NINE
THE DEVIL
AND THE DEMONS

Mark 1:21–39 _____ Luke 4:31–44

WE ARE ALREADY FAMILIAR WITH THE WORDS "SATAN"
(Mark 1:13) and "devil" (Luke 4:2ff) in the exposition of the
gospel. Jesus established his personal ascendancy over the devil in
his temptations in the wilderness; he is now to carry that victory
into his public ministry. The New Testament makes frequent
reference to demons and/or unclean spirits, and Jesus is reported
to have dealt with them on a number of occasions. Our text in
Mark's Gospel records one such meeting. Since there is a wide
variety of views held in this connection, and a great uncertainty
prevails on the subject—even among Christians—we must at-
tempt a few words of clarification.

Our own generation judges itself to be too sophisticated to
believe seriously in the devil. For many, reference to Satan and
his work seems extremely naïve, even quaint. Unable to distinguish clearly between demon possession and the occult, between
incantation and the authoritative Word of God, between magic
and healing, we tend to ignore both as equally primitive and
ingenuous. Yet to dismiss the more than forty references in the
New Testament to Satan, the devil, the evil one, and the Antichrist so casually is inconsistent with reputable scholarship.

Satan, or the devil, is the inclusive name given to the powers
of evil abroad in the world which permeate all the activities,
institutions, and undertakings of the human race. Other names
are used, usually to suggest certain characteristics: "tempter,"
"Antichrist," "mocker," "destroyer," "unclean spirit," "the
enemy." "According to the Bible, the principalities are legion in
species, number, variety and name.... They are designated by

such multifarious titles as power, virtues, thrones, dominions, demons, princes, strongholds, lords, angels, gods, elements, spirits. Sometimes the names of other creatures are appropriated for them, such as serpent, dragon, lion, beast" (William Stringfellow, *An Ethic for Christians and Other Aliens in a Strange Land*; Waco, TX: Word Books, 1973, pp. 77f). In this sense a principality may be defined as that, of whatever nature, which assumes, grasps, or exercises any power or authority or influence; or in which power, authority, and/or influence may be said to inhere.

Demons—themselves forces of evil—are the messengers of Satan as his "angels" (Matt. 25:41; 2 Cor. 12:7; Rev. 12:7). Angels (of God) and demons stand in relationship to one another—a relationship which is always one of radical opposition—as creation and chaos, good and evil, life and death, redemption and perdition. The devil is that power, and collectively those powers standing in opposition to God's purposes, work, and rule in the world for the good and well-being of his creation—seeking to subvert, nullify, cancel, and overthrow all that God does for the benefit of his people. The basic tool of Satan's trade is falsehood; he is a liar and the father of lies (John 8:44).

The New Testament does not ask its readers to *believe* in the devil; nor has the church done so. The devil is not an object of faith. Nevertheless, he is there—improperly there, illegitimately there, irrationally there; there as the single power aligned against God, and as the origin and source of all the forces seeking to annul the work and purpose of God in the world.

We have now to inquire of the nature of evil and of the principalities of which we have been speaking. We have indicated that, according to the New Testament, "devil" is the comprehensive term used to signify the presence of evil in the world, such that we may also speak of "devils," "power," "elements," etc. We now ask whether "devil" and/or "Satan" is properly designated an abstraction, a principle, an influence, or as in some sense personal, creaturely—an entity.

There can be no question of the way in which the New Testament answers our problem. From the very beginning—the temptations of Jesus—the devil is referred to as a living thing, a form of life. The demons speak to Jesus, and he in turn commands and rebukes them. There would be little point in rebuking an abstraction. Here is a partial list of references in which the forces of evil are unmistakably seen as creatures having their own existence: Matt. 9:33, 34; 17:18; Mark 1:34, 3:25, 7:29; Luke 4:41, 9:42. Yet for many of us it is only with the greatest reluctance that we accord personhood (i.e. entity) to the devil. For moderns to do so seems archaic, quaint, and even gullible. That the devil is an abstraction, that he has no genuine existence, that he does not therefore warrant being taken seriously, is doubtless one of his principal lies.

*   *   *

The first sign (miracle) recorded by Mark (1:23-26) concerns a man with an unclean spirit that made its appearance in the synagogue at Capernaum. We are not told the external symptoms which made our Lord's diagnosis possible. Indeed, it seems the spirit revealed itself by addressing Jesus as it did. Had the evil spirit not spoken, its presence might have gone undetected. Or again, something in Jesus' teaching, referred to in vv. 21 and 22, may have aroused the spirit to protest. Finally, it may have been the authoritative way in which Jesus taught that not only impressed his listeners, but also convinced the evil spirit that it was in the presence of one whose power was invincible.

It should come as no surprise to learn that a man troubled by an unclean spirit should be found "in the synagogue." Churchgoers are not immune to the wiles of the devil. Indeed, church may be the very place where more people, similarly afflicted, *should* be found, in the hope of hearing an authentic word of the Lord which would set them free. In any event, it is worth our passing notice that Jesus did not expel the worshiper from the synagogue; he expelled the evil spirit from the man. Those who had gathered in the synagogue, already "astonished" at his teaching, were "amazed" at his exorcism. Although the Jews were presumably familiar with exorcism, Mark's point evidently is that Jesus' exorcisms were not like any others they had seen before.

After the incident in the synagogue Jesus entered the home of

Simon and Andrew, where Simon's mother-in-law lay sick. The object of his mission was the same: to exhibit the power of the new age which had dawned with his coming. The earlier cure he had accomplished with a word of command; he healed Simon's mother-in-law by an act of grace.

Jesus' presence in Capernaum and his apparent approachability was just too good an opportunity for the townspeople to miss: "That evening at sundown (at which time it was lawful for sufferers to be on the streets) they brought to him all who were sick or possessed with demons." The types of illness were "various"; and the demons no doubt diverse. Mark's intention is evidently to stress the universality of Jesus' power to heal, regardless of the nature of the diseases and afflictions from which the people were suffering.

*   *   *

As we read the gospel records, we encounter stories of healing, of the restoration of sight and other faculties, and the recalling to life of those who have died. Such narratives, though diverse, have one aspect in common. For the most part they are told of people or groups of people. This might easily lead us to believe that the possession of demons, evil spirits, and the like is always a personal and in some respects a private thing. Modern parallels may be observed in such afflictions as alcoholism, the gambling fever, drug addiction, sexual perversion, and a propensity to outbursts of violent temper—to mention only a few examples. Yet the scope and magnitude of the demonic is not confined to the individual. We may acquire some insight into the devastation wrought by mass demon possession in the story (Luke 8:26–32) of the exorcism in the country of the Gerasenes in which the demons, expelled from the man bound and fettered, entered into swine. We see it again—this time in an almost institutionalized form—during Jesus' trial before Pilate, when the people wittingly chose to crucify innocence rather than proven guilt (Matt. 27:23b *et al.*).

Paul probably did more than any other New Testament writer to expand our knowledge and understanding of the subject with his use of the word "principalities" to describe the enormous implications of the power of evil (Rom. 8:38; Ephes. 1:21, 3:10, 6:12; Col. 1:16, 2:15). From this we may learn that evil is more than a force; it has some of the characteristics and attributes of a realm, of a *regime*. Evil seeks to rule, to govern as a malevolent alternative to the kingdom of God. As Stringfellow has observed, some of the words used in the Bible to designate the principalities are (or seem) quaint; if we interpret them in contemporary language they lose their quaintness, and the principalities become recognizable and all too familiar: institutions, ideologies, images, movements, causes, corporations, bureaucracies, traditions, methods, conglomerates, governments, and idols. Thus capitalism, Maoism, humanism, astrology, science, white supremacy, money, sex, patriotism, technology, family—and others almost without number—are or can be governed by principalities. Principalities are included among God's creatures (Col. 1:16), and suffer from the Fall as truly as do human beings. They falsely claim autonomy from God and dominion over human beings and over the rest of creation.

*　　　　*　　　　*

Throughout the earlier chapters on the life and ministry of Jesus, consistent references have been made to our Lord in what may appear to be the most extravagant terms. He has been described as the fulfillment of the promise made by God to Abraham, the historical realization of two thousand years of Hebrew prophecy, the visible verification of the faithfulness of Israel's God, the Son of God and Savior of the world, and the "Messiah." We have even joined the author of the letter to the Hebrews in saying that Jesus has "destroyed him who has the power of death, that is, the devil."

Can this be possible? Is it true? When we look around us we find little, if any, confirmation of these claims. We see instead that evil persists, even flourishes: crime increases, there is no real cessation of war in the world, the society in which we live is marked by a sharp decline in the quality of life, men and women continue to lie and cheat and steal. In short, nothing seems to have changed. How then can we speak of the conquest of evil?

We speak as we do quite simply because, in full awareness of the gravity of the situation, Jesus spoke the same way: "In the world you have tribulation; but be of good cheer, I have overcome the world" (John 16:33); and we believe his witness is true. We believe, with Paul, that Jesus sits "at his (God's) right hand in heavenly places, far above all rule and authority and power and dominion . . . and that he (God) has put all things under his (Christ's) feet . . . (Ephes. 1:21f); and that he (God) "disarmed the principalities and powers, and made a public example of them, triumphing over them in him (Christ)" (Col. 2:15). The Book of Revelation was written during the period of unremitting persecution of the church, yet its basic theme is, "The Lord God Omnipotent Reigneth" (Handel's *Messiah*; from Rev. 19:6). By this, we are impressed.

Nevertheless, *why* do we believe it? Paul wrote (1 Cor. 15:26) that "the last enemy that shall be destroyed is death": the last, not only chronologically, but in the sense that until death itself had been put to death no one would be free from its power; and conversely, once death had been conquered, mankind's freedom would be realized. This is precisely what has taken place in our Lord's resurrection. And "by his great mercy we have been born anew to a living hope through the resurrection of Jesus Christ from the dead" (1 Peter 1:3). When Jesus said from the cross, "It is finished," we may understand him to have meant, "My work is completed and accomplished."

The new age co-exists in tension with the old. The kingdom of God competes with the kingdoms of this world for the hearts and minds of men and women. The Spirit continues to war against the flesh. But the decisive battle has already been fought and won by Jesus Christ our Lord, and nothing can separate us from the love of God found in him. Even death lacks that power. The devil knows his time is short, and we have nothing to fear.

The connection between the expulsion of the unclean spirit from the man in the synagogue and the resurrection of Jesus from the dead is direct. It was by the same power—Jesus once called it "the finger of God"—that both miracles were accomplished. The first sign demonstrated Jesus' complete mastery over the evil spirit; the second proclaimed his conquest of the principality of death.

Meanwhile, we live in a period of time when the ages—the

new and the old—overlap. The death warrant of death and the devil has been signed by God and sealed by Jesus Christ. With confidence we await the outcome, knowing that "because he lives, we shall live also."

TEN

THE POWER
OF RESTORATION

Mark 5:21–43 ————————————————— Luke 7:1–23

THE SCRIPTURE PASSAGES NOTED ABOVE BRING TOGETHER four of the most celebrated of Jesus' mighty works. They have been brought together with a purpose: that upon completing our study we may have no remaining doubt that Jesus is indeed *Lord*; i.e. that he governs in his own right. Every one of these narratives, taken singly, warrants closer attention than we can give in one chapter, for our present objective is, in some sense, to see our Lord's ministry whole.

Within the Christian church (and outside it as well), the English-speaking people of the world have a deep commitment to the word "miracle." This is probably a residual legacy from our 450-year exclusive use of the Authorized, or King James Version of the Bible. In that translation (1611) the word "miracle" occurs 30 times, doing service for both the Greek words in the original: *dunameis* means acts of power; and *semeia* means signs. The Revised Standard Version (1946) is in this respect more service-able; the word "miracle" occurs only seven times, and never as a translation of the word *semeia*. The significance of this change is readily appreciated. The King James Version puts primary em-phasis on the miraculous nature of Jesus' work; its significance is subordinated. The word "miracle" by itself is neutral; it may denote magic, the occult, or mere entertainment. The question, Do you believe in miracles? may be, and often is, simply a test of your credulity, having nothing whatever to do with faith in Jesus Christ. Indeed it is more than likely that we all believe in mira-cles, loosely defined. That is to say, we believe in the reality of those things that happen in daily life for which we have no logical or rational explanation. ("It's a miracle he wasn't killed." "We never expected to see her alive again.") The question posed by the New Testament, however, is this: Do you believe that Jesus' works of mercy are signs of the new age? or, Do you discern in the ministry of Jesus evidence of a new and unique power which, in its mastery over sickness and death, bears witness to the presence of the Messiah? That question was uppermost in John's mind as he sat in prison contemplating the teaching and healing of our Lord (Luke 3:19, 7:19).

It is most important that we understand who and what Jesus is, as distinct from his characteristics, and prior to and independent of our confession of him. Jesus is Lord, and *our* Lord whether we acknowledge him as such or not. He is not only our Lord, but *the* Lord—Lord, for example, of sickness and disease, of life and death. His position as Lord is not merely titular or honorary. He is so in reality and in fact. He rules: he heals, he cures, he raises from the the dead. His Lordship does not await our confession of it; we do not, by our confession, make him Lord. Sickness and death are subject to him: or better, they are his subjects, his slaves. They obey him (as the Roman centurion was quick to observe). They serve him, as the illness of the woman (Mark 5:25) and the death of the maiden (v. 35) were made to serve Jesus' witness to himself as Lord. The illness of the centurion's servant and the death of the son of the widow of Nain accomplish the same purpose in Luke's narrative.

It seems superfluous to devote a paragraph to emphasizing the sympathetic way in which Jesus treated the people. Surely no one could regard with such kindness and concern the lame, the blind, the poor, the destitute, and the wrongheaded without evoking compassion. Apparently Jesus had time to spend with everyone regardless of age, nationality, or station in life. He embraced the children; he responded to the plea of the Roman centurion; he spoke to the Syro-Phoenician woman; he fed the multitude; he enlisted Zacchaeus; he wept over the city of Jerusalem; and he forthrightly addressed himself to the dead! Such compassion has not been seen before or since.

Serious illness is frequently the precursor of death. Accordingly, in all four narratives before us death is either present or at hand. In each of the episodes Jesus was dealing with the most powerful of all the principalities, the most implacable and malevolent of all his enemies. It was perhaps his clear understanding of the nature of the adversary, together with a thorough appreciation of human helplessness, that accounts for the depth of his compassion and his infinite tenderness.

*   *   *

It would be easy enough to exhort and encourage the Christian community to follow Jesus' example in the matter of compassion. Surely, in these later years of the twentieth century, there are few Christian virtues more to be desired and less in evidence. Ours has been called a "violent society," and not without good reason. Exhortations of this nature have not been lacking; yet they seem to have made little impression. In many quarters human compassion appears to have lost much of its impetus, and its practice is fitful at best.

Jesus has provided us with the perfect example for our attitudes to people in need and distress. Unfailingly kind, considerate, gentle, and deeply concerned, he is the perfect model for our conduct and outlook. He is, indeed, the Great Teacher proclaimed by an earlier generation.

The question remains, however: Did Jesus heal the sick, restore sight to the blind, cleanse the leper, and raise the dead *for these reasons*: i.e. to provide us with an example and a model? To answer in the affirmative may suggest perhaps without our realizing it that Jesus was "putting on an act" for our benefit. It seems rather that the example Jesus has set for us was almost incidental and inadvertent—a by-product of his primary love and concern for the people of his own day.

In the final analysis, following an example or conforming to a model can be a pretty mechanical undertaking. It need have no impetus or motivation beyond itself. It is perhaps commendable as an exercise in tenacity and endurance, but in it is no spontaneity and no joy. It cannot "run and not be weary" nor "walk and not faint" (Isa. 40:31b).

Jesus' actions and attitudes witnessed powerfully to his relationship to God and his identity with mankind. Convinced as he was of his own Sonship, he was also persuaded of our weakness and need of grace. In retrospect he could have repeated the words from John's Gospel: "God so loved the world . . . ." He saw and understood his contemporaries as the children of the Father—of *his* Father, and therefore the objects of his love. Ignorant children, wayward children, misguided and perverse children—but children nonetheless: his own brothers and sisters, indeed his own flesh and blood (John 1:14). This conviction, we may be sure, provided the well-spring of Jesus' compassion and his obedience.

It cannot be otherwise with us. Our attitudes and actions also (for good or ill) proclaim our relationship to God and our oneness with all mankind. Are they, or are they not, our brothers and sisters in Christ? Are we, or are we not, prepared to receive and accept our Lord's two-fold stricture: "Truly, I say to you, as you did it (not) to one of the least of these my brethren, you did it (not) to me" (Matt. 25)? The well-spring of Christian compassion is therefore seen to be the realization of our common humanity, our common need, and that in Christ there is one God and Father of us all.

*   *   *

The relationship of faith to healing is a subject to be treated with the utmost reserve and even caution. Too often we have been known to jump to a conclusion, most frequently the same one: if you believe you will be healed. The corollary is that if you do not believe you have no right to ask, and you are not likely to be heard anyway. Surely this is a simplistic caricature of the teaching of the New Testament on this matter. If such were the faith of the church, it would lead to the most irresponsible bargaining imaginable. ("Dear God, if you will heal my son, restore my daughter, spare my wife, I will believe in you.") Moreover, it distorts the very nature of faith itself, where faith becomes *my* work and *my* accomplishment, which I then "give" in return for God's favor and favorable treatment.

In the four narratives to hand, three of the recipients of grace are commended or encouraged for their faith; in connection with the widow of Nain there is no mention of it. There are other accounts of Jesus' mighty deeds in which no reference is made to the faith of the petitioner. A notable example is the story (Luke 17) of the healing of the ten lepers. We are left to conclude in that instance that only one of them could be said to have faith.

God's favor in healing, restoration, renewal, and relief (e.g. from pain) appears therefore to be bestowed almost at random. It has no discernible pattern; it is unpredictable. Like the rain, it falls "on the just and the unjust" (Matt. 5:45). We ought not to conclude, however, that God does not know what he is doing. We may be sure that what appears indiscriminate to us is exceedingly purposeful with him. But we know this only because we know him!

*   *   *

Have you found the foregoing discussions of Jesus' ministry a bit difficult to understand? Have you come away from them a little puzzled? Take heart; John was also perplexed by what he had heard in prison of Jesus' ministry. He sought a flat, forthright statement from Jesus, to be transmitted by his (John's) disciples, saying: "Look no further; I am the Messiah," or conversely, "Do not jump to conclusions; the Messiah has yet to come." As we have already seen, John did not get his answer.

In this connection there are three possible explanations. (a) The deeply personal nature of the decision to believe. Jesus may have been alert to the weakness of the argument: "He is my Savior and my Lord, and the Messiah, for he himself has said so." (b) In view of current conflicting views of the role of the Messiah, Jesus may have wished to avoid the possibility of his claim being misunderstood in nationalistic, political, and/or military terms. (c) John's question was posed in the early stages of Jesus' ministry. Our Lord was unwilling, as yet, to face public charges of claiming to be the Messiah. He still had much to do and teach.

*   *   *

An elder of the Kirk, aged about 70 years, enters the hospital where tests reveal a cancerous condition in the region of the spine.* He undergoes surgery for relief of the ailment; but sub-

*The incidents recorded in this section are matters of personal knowledge to the writer.

sequent examination shows that the cancer has spread throughout his body. He is given cobalt-ray treatment. In due time he is discharged from the hospital, but reports back for periodic examination. Eventually, the tests reveal not a trace of cancer remaining in his system.

A twelve-year-old girl is brought to the hospital suffering frequent headaches, nausea, and double vision. Tests and X-rays disclose a tumor centered in the area of the brain (whether malignant or not is not specified). The youngster undergoes surgery to relieve pressure on the brain; but the location of the growth makes it inoperable. Her minister asks the congregation for their prayers—public and private. In lieu of further surgery, cobalt-ray treatment is prescribed. Not long thereafter the patient is discharged, returns to school and, having missed three months of instruction, leads her class in mathematics. Subsequent brain scans show only the scar where the growth had been. She is one of three such patients to have recovered in the long history of that medical institution.

A telephone call is received late on Sunday evening. The caller's wife has been several weeks in the hospital with spinal problems, and in spite of all that can be done for her, she has been in constant and excruciating pain. Prayers are requested. On Monday morning at eight o'clock the pain has ceased. Released from the hospital a few days later, she has had no recurrence of pain.

If we could account in medical terms for the recovery of these patients, would that explain away the "miracle"? Or would these incidents still be "miracles"? Surely we have passed the stage of finding evidence of the presence of God only in things we cannot understand, so that God appears to become less relevant as our knowledge increases. God does not depend on our ignorance for his security.

Unmistakably the teaching of the New Testament is that during his earthly ministry Jesus had complete power and authority over sickness and death. Are we to suppose that Jesus, now risen, no longer possesses this power? On the contrary, there is no diminution of Jesus' powers as the risen Christ, and no tempering or mitigation of his Lordship. "Let all the house of Israel know assuredly that God has made him both Lord and Christ, this Jesus whom you crucified" (Acts 2:36). The risen Christ continues to be Lord; he continues, as it were *in absentia*, to do his mighty works. The claim that certain of these mighty works are miracles involves an interpretation, which in part depends on our definition of the word "miracle." The Christian church sees them above all as *signs*, the occasion for which did not end with the close of our Lord's ministry on earth.

The practice of medicine? Let us just say that God permits the doctors (and others) to share in his work of healing, and has graciously made us his partners in compassion. It is a modest, yet proud, claim.

ELEVEN
THE POWER
OF FORGIVENESS

Mark 2:1–12 _____ Luke 7:36–50

IT IS INTERESTING, THOUGH NOT ALTOGETHER SURPRISING,
that in two contemporary rock operas with biblical themes the
most successful and thoughtfully moving solos are concerned
with Jesus' power to forgive sin. Both are assigned to women,
and in both instances the soloist is evidently Mary Magdalene. In
Jesus Christ, Superstar, the woman who sings "I Don't Know
How to Love Him" is the woman who has "had so many men
before in very many ways." Yet, confronted by Jesus, she finds
herself in emotional disarray and indecision, not knowing
whether to advance or retreat, or how to conduct herself. On the
one hand, "he scares me so"; on the other, "I love him so." This
paradoxical reaction to Jesus is consistent with the observation of
the psalmist that "there is forgiveness with thee, that thou
mayest be *feared*" (130:4). In *A Man Dies* (E.M.I.; England),
Mary Magdalene, upon learning that Jesus has been crucified,
misunderstands his death and abandons all hope of forgiveness
and salvation. She can only sing of "Blues in the Night" such
that "friends can't comfort me."

Both of the stories focused upon here have to do with the
forgiveness of sin. The one text tells of an incident that took place
in the home of a Pharisee. The other relates an episode which
occurred in the presence of "some of the scribes." In both cases,
the on-lookers had the utmost difficulty in understanding what
took place and condoning Jesus' attitude toward it. Yet all of these
men and women shared with Jesus the religion and traditions of
Judaism which was their common heritage.

The Pharisees probably originated in the period before the

Maccabean War, in resistance to the Hellenizing influence of those who wished to adopt Greek customs. In opposing this trend they derived their strength from the Mosaic Law, strictly adhering to it. The fierce persecution of the Jews by a Syrian overlord, Antiochus Epiphanes, between 175–162 B.C., further consolidated their party; and some of the most prominent men in Jewish history of the time were members of it. As Pharisaism developed, however, it became increasingly legalistic—that interpretation which makes religion rigidly conform to the Law, and promises God's grace only to those who obey it implicitly. Religion then inevitably becomes external. The disposition of the heart is of less importance than the outward act. It culminates in self-congratulatory righteousness.

Unlike the Pharisee, the scribe was not a member of a sect or party; the word denotes an occupation. A scribe was a copier of the law and of other parts of Scripture. Later, they began also to interpret the law and to study its application to daily life. The decisions of the great scribes became the oral law, or tradition. There were, among the scribes, some who believed in Jesus' teaching (e.g. Matt. 8:19), but these were exceptions. Their preoccupation with the law had seemingly made it difficult for them to be anything but legalistic.

Accordingly, in the two stories before us concerning forgiveness, we find Jesus confronting representatives of the hard core of opposition to his ministry—members of two factions which will ultimately exert a decisive influence in bringing about his death.

Seen from one point of view, forgiveness is highly intangible: it can neither be demonstrated conclusively nor verified empirically. Yet (if we may say so) it will not go away. One indication of this is the furor aroused among the religious people by Jesus' claim to be able to forgive sins—a claim which was in many respects a major cause of his death. A corroborating circumstance is evident, we believe, in modern society: the absence (or ignorance) of forgiveness works havoc with the human psyche. Many a guilt-ridden soul has been tortured beyond the limits of endurance because of a failure to believe, or an ignorance of, the free offer of grace through Jesus Christ. At this point perhaps, the prospective rapprochement between psychology and theology so widely heralded today may help to relieve the tension of guilt.

Nevertheless we must be persuaded that the forgiveness of sin emphatically does not consist in such vacuous remarks as, "Think nothing of it," or "Don't take it too seriously."

In Mark's account of the healing of the paralytic, when the scribes "questioned within themselves," it is apparent that they objected to Jesus' assuming authority to forgive sin on God's behalf; they were horrified and incensed at his boldness. We understand their reaction better if we reflect on the seriousness attributed to sin by Jewish tradition. (Comp. e.g. Isa. 53; and in the Psalms, 32:1-7, 51, 90:8, and others.) The same sentiments were expressed, somewhat less forcefully, by the Pharisee's guests as recorded in Luke's narrative. And in one respect both were right. It *does* belong to God alone to forgive sins. We, like the Pharisees and scribes, must make up our minds: Jesus is either the Messiah, with the authority to forgive sins, or he is an imposter. There is no third way.

We have mentioned that the genuineness of the forgiveness of sins cannot be confirmed in any empirical way. Instead, Jesus offered to the scribes visible evidence, not of forgiveness, but of his unique powers—indeed, of his Messiahship. They seem to have concurred ("We never saw anything like this!"), but whether, as a result, they believed him to be the Christ of God is not stated.

"Sin" is not a word often used outside church circles. Generally speaking, concepts of right and wrong are formed in the light of commonly held standards of moral conduct, personal and social. The principles by which right and wrong may be established have no necessary relationship to religious conviction. Persons having little or no discernible faith sometimes have a very strict and well-defined code of ethics. Standards of morality, however, are not the same in every place and age, varying from country to country, and from one century (or even decade) to the next. The so-called "new morality" is a recent example of the flexibility of standards of human conduct and attitudes which do not have their roots in anything more substantial than human pride, caprice, or consensus.

Christian faith, however, puts the issues of right and wrong in the wholly different context of God's will for his people. It is more deeply concerned with sin and righteousness than with human conduct solely on the level of ethics. Strictly speaking, an ethical system can make no provision for its ultimate inadequacy and failure: it knows nothing of forgiveness and redemption because it knows nothing of God. In the realm of pure ethics, the psalmist's question, "If thou, O Lord, shouldst mark iniquities, Lord, who could stand?" (130:3) would never arise. Accordingly, it is little wonder that there is so much "guilt-edged" neurosis abroad in society today. In spite of all our brave assertions of a new-found freedom from the shackles of traditional morality, our lot has scarcely improved. Only God's truth can make us truly free.

*   *   *

In Luke's account of the "woman who was a sinner," Jesus' authoritative declaration, "Your sins are forgiven," comes almost as an anticlimax. In retrospect we can see that forgiveness had already been granted before Jesus pronounced it. The actions of the woman immediately upon entering the Pharisee's house are consistent with those of one who has sinned greatly and accepted gladly the forgiveness which Jesus preached. Her tears were tears of gratitude rather than remorse, and so were more precious than the ointment with which she anointed his feet. The woman was not trying to earn forgiveness, nor to pay for it. Hers was simply a grandiose gesture of sheer gratitude. Had she been asked to give an account of her actions she could not have done better than to quote the psalmist: "I love the Lord because he has heard my voice and my supplications" (116:1).

The consequences for the forgiven Christian's conduct and attitudes are enormous. Luke's Gospel (6:37b) contains our Lord's brief, direct statement: "forgive, and you will be forgiven." Note, however, that the statement is positive; the converse, i.e. "if you do not forgive, you will not be forgiven," is lacking. Jesus wishes to govern by teaching and exhortation, not by threat. The obligation to forgive is laid upon us as recipients of the mercy of God. "Be merciful, even as your Father is merciful" (6:36).

Let it be said that our forgiveness of the offenses of others does not come easily, and it certainly does not come naturally.

Why should it? Jesus' forgiveness of us cost him his life. When in *An Essay on Criticism* Alexander Pope wrote: "To err is human; to forgive, divine," he was pointing in the right direction. Divinity is not one of our natural attributes. Yet it is to this grace that we are called.

According to the New Testament, our forgiveness of others is not grounded in our own temperaments, inclinations, or frames of mind. These indeed are capricious and unpredictable. Nor is it merely a matter of following Jesus' example. "You have received without pay, give without pay" (K.J.V.: "freely ye have received, freely give," Matt. 10:8). This may be said to apply to forgiveness as to other Christian gifts. Jesus' commandment to forgive others, and therefore that forgiveness be a conspicuous characteristic of the community called by his name, is grounded in God's forgiveness of our sin. The church is called, not only to be the forgiven (redeemed) community; it is called also, consequently, to be the forgiving community, as is clear from the parable of the debtor recorded in Matt. 18:23ff (where there is a threat). There is a direct connection between our having received free pardon of all our sins and our willingness to "forgive your brother from your hearts" (v. 35).

"Don't worry about it," is a poor substitute for genuine forgiveness. When Jesus taught his disciples that if your brother "sins against you seven times in the day, and turns to you seven times, and says, 'I repent,' you must forgive him" (Luke 17:4), the disciples began to appreciate with what seriousness he spoke. (In the parallel passage in Matthew's Gospel, the figure is four hundred and ninety; there is no mention of forgiveness per day.) The disciples respond with awe: "Increase our faith." When Peter asked (comp. Matthew) how often one should forgive, he was asking for a rule of thumb with which he might conceivably comply. Jesus' reply turned the matter around by giving him a "rule of heart." Instead of saying, "This is what you have to do," Jesus said, in effect, "This is the kind of person I want you to be."

That you and I and the whole Christian community should be in constant, unbroken harmony with one another is of the utmost importance to God. Indeed, where such harmony with our brothers and sisters does not exist, our relationship with God himself is in jeopardy. "So if you are offering your gift at the altar, and there remember that your brother has something against you, leave your gift there before the altar and go; first be reconciled to your brother, and then come and offer your gift" (Matt. 5:23f). Worship is largely vitiated if we are "out of charity" with our contemporaries. We may feel that it has done a lot of good, or that "it was good for us to have been (there)"; but God is not deceived and knows when our worship is vain.

We must also face the possibility, indeed the probability, that many people do in fact withhold their forgiveness of offenses. They cannot bring themselves to be reconciled to their brethren, and remain aloof. We think immediately of the elder brother in the parable of the prodigal son (Luke 15:11–32). In this story there is no indication that the elder son was not exactly what he said he was—a man of highest principles, faithful and constant in fulfilling all his duties. He was entitled to a good deal of respect. We are probably right in saying that his outstanding characteristic was rectitude—that irritating habit that some people have of always being right, and knowing it. We may be assured that it was precisely his uprightness, and consciousness of it, that prevented this man from receiving his younger brother with joy and gladness. At this point we find ourselves back again thinking of the (legalism of) the Pharisees and scribes, for the story was told to them (v. 2). Does the Father continue to love this unlovable son? We may believe that the elder brother has, by failing to be reconciled to the prodigal, placed in jeopardy his own standing in the family of the Father. By his intransigence he is teetering on the brink of exclusion from the family circle. Nevertheless, the Father seeks to reassure him. He will no more give up on the elder son than he did on the prodigal. "Son, you are always with me, and all that is mine is yours" (v. 31). There is forgiveness for the Pharisees of this world, too.

TWELVE

THE POWER TO TRANSFORM

Mark 8:34–38 _____ Luke 19:1–10

LET US BEGIN BY QUOTING A BRIEF PARAGRAPH FROM AN earlier chapter:

> The new age co-exists in tension with the old. The kingdom of God competes with the kingdoms of this world for the hearts and minds of men and women. The spirit continues to war against the flesh. But the decisive battle has already been fought and won by Jesus Christ our Lord. Nothing can separate us from the love of God found in him. Even death lacks that power. The devil knows his time is short, and we have nothing to fear.

And again,

> Meanwhile, we live in a period of time when the ages—the old and the new—overlap.

The apostle Paul uses similar language to express and expound what the coming of the new age means for the individual. His vocabulary is variously translated in the New Testament as follows: The King James Version gives us words such as "the old man" and "the new man"; "carnally minded" and "spiritually minded"; "the natural man" and "the spiritual man"; "he that is carnal" and "he that is spiritual." The Revised Standard Version gives us "the old self," "the old nature," and "the new nature"; he who "sets his mind on the flesh," and "he who sets his mind on the spirit"; "the unspiritual man" and "the spiritual man"; they who are "of the flesh" and they who are "of the spirit." More often than not, Paul sets these pairs of expressions over against one another, thus both linking them together and differentiating between them.

It is plain, especially in the letter to the Romans, that the two "natures" co-exist, and even overlap, in the Christian believer. Paul has given a vivid portrayal of the conflict between them in chapters seven and eight of that epistle. Men and women, upon becoming Christian, are not thereby immediately perfected; rather they have but entered upon that struggle against sin so convincingly described in these chapters. Paul seems to say, "you win some, you lose some; but you never give up." That is why he is "wretched" and longs for someone who will deliver him "from this body of death."

*   *   *

The Jews, as a conquered people, were obliged to pay tribute to the Roman authorities. The right to enforce this tax in a given region was put up for auction. Subsequently, those who bought this right might sub-contract with others for the privilege in more restricted areas. The chief tax-collectors were usually Romans of high social standing; the sub-contract was normally let to Jews. The New Testament calls this latter class "publicans," from the Latin "pertaining to public revenue." With a few notable exceptions these subordinate tax-gatherers were extortioners (Luke 3:12f), thoroughly despised by their own people. A new word for traitor was coined during the Second World War—a "quisling"—the name of a man who co-operated with the enemy against his native land. Zacchaeus was one of them; Matthew had been another.

When Paul wrote to the Romans (12:2) urging them not to be "conformed to this world, but (to be) transformed by the renewing of (their) mind," he was referring to an experience such as Zacchaeus had undergone. It was comparable to that which had overtaken Paul himself on the Damascus road. Others had experienced a similar change, many of them anonymous in the New Testament.

The facets of human life are almost without number, yet none goes completely untouched by the power of Christian conversion. "If any man be in Christ, he is a new creature . . . behold *all* things are become new" (preferring, for the moment, the

K.J.V. rendering of 2 Cor. 5:17). They become new, not because of any change in the objective, external world, but because of the change wrought by the Spirit of God in the hearts and minds of converts. Quite literally, nothing the world has to offer looks the same to the "new nature" as it did to the "old nature." Human conduct and attitudes, values and judgments, hopes and aspirations, perspectives and priorities, all are subjected to the most radical questioning and the most profound change when Christians know that they are not their own, having been "bought with a price" (1 Cor. 6:20); they are therefore no longer alone at the center of their own lives, and no longer solely at their own disposal. Their desires and ambitions must give place to the will of the God who made and redeemed them.

Paul's eloquent pleading and frequent exhortations to the members of the earliest Christian communities strongly emphasize Christian obedience and the new life in Christ. Though he may sometimes sound like a legislator bringing forth a new code of law, he is far from that. Rather, he emphasizes the breadth and depth of the new life to which his hearers (readers) have been called in Jesus Christ. He does not mince words, nor does he spare feelings. "Let us then cast off the works of darkness and put on the armor of light; let us conduct ourselves becomingly as in the day, not in reveling and drunkenness, not in debauchery and licentiousness, not in quarreling and jealousy. But put on the Lord Jesus Christ, and make no provision for the flesh, to gratify its desires" (Rom. 13:12b–14). "But I say, walk by the Spirit, and do not gratify the desires of the flesh. . . . Now the works of the flesh are plain: immorality, impurity, licentiousness, idolatry, sorcery, enmity, strife, jealousy, anger, self-ishness, dissension, party spirit, envy, drunkenness, carousing, and the like . . . but the fruit of the Spirit is love, joy, peace, patience, kindness, goodness, faithfulness, gentleness, self-control; against such there is no law" (Gal. 5:16, 19–21, 22–23). These exhortations, of which we never cease to stand in need, are continued in the pastoral epistles.

From the apparent chronological sequence in which the story of Zacchaeus appears in Luke's Gospel—the eighteenth of twenty-four chapters—we may judge that Jesus' ministry was fairly well advanced. By this time he was reasonably well known. In the somewhat limited area to which he had confined his ministry, not everyone had seen him, but many had. Many more, of whom Zacchaeus was one, had heard of him.

Jesus took the initiative: he placed himself in Zacchaeus' debt by inviting himself to be the publican's guest. The obviousness with which our Lord did this indicates that this was no chance encounter. Zacchaeus (all unsuspecting?) was delighted to be so conspicuously singled out to play host to a celebrity. He climbed rapidly down from his perch and presented himself to Jesus. The onlookers grumbled; but Zacchaeus was used to that, and Jesus did not care. For a moment or two (we may suppose) not a word was exchanged between them. Then, suddenly, Zacchaeus crumbled. "Behold, Lord, the half of my goods I give to the poor. . . ." This greedy, avaricious, self-serving "quisling" had broken down. Zacchaeus did not need Jesus to *tell* him that he was a liar, cheat, and a thief. Our Lord's presence was enough. There is something about Jesus that renders us completely defenseless of our sins without a word being spoken. (Comp. Luke 5:8— "Depart from me, for I am a sinful man, O Lord.")

One half of Zacchaeus' possessions will be given to the poor. From the remaining half he will reimburse, four to one, those from whom he has stolen. His reversal was dramatic indeed. The "four-fold" may have been in accordance with prevailing Roman law regarding restitution in cases of theft; or perhaps in compliance with an Old Testament penalty for stealing sheep (Exod. 22:1). In either case Zacchaeus' intention is clearly a frank admission of guilt; it is also evidence of his genuine repentance.

If we are not careful to make the necessary distinctions, we might be misled by Jesus' comment on this incident. We might conclude from Jesus' words that Zacchaeus had earned salvation by his gifts to the poor and his program of reimbursement. Nothing could be further from the truth. Salvation came to Zacchaeus, not because he was going to give everything back, but because of the change of heart by which he himself was restored as truly a son of Abraham, i.e. as one truly belonging to the heritage of Israel.

Luke tells us that Zacchaeus was looking for Jesus, trying to see him. Jesus says that he was looking for men such as Zacchaeus, to save them. Zacchaeus was apparently curious; Jesus was deeply concerned.

The theme of the Bible from beginning to end is God's activity in relentless pursuit of his intention to reconcile the world unto himself. Men and women, by their original nature children of God, have become estranged, separated, and rebellious against him. Nevertheless, God will not leave it at that; he is not content to be at loggerheads with those whom he loves. He longs to bring us back to fellowship with him. It is for this reason that he called Abraham out of Ur in the first place. It was with this in mind that his promise to Abraham (and to his descendants) was made. It was for this purpose that in calling Abraham he founded (created) a people. Among Abraham's children, and his children's children, the bearer of the promise was designated in each generation—Isaac, Jacob (Israel), and Judah. He in whom all nations of the earth would be blessed would come from the tribe bearing Judah's name. Israel would be uniquely God's people— the servant-nation of the Lord. Accordingly God gave them laws, prophets, and priests to keep alive the hope of their redemption, to remind them constantly of their special place in his plan of salvation, and of their special duty to him. He tried them and tested them, he counselled and comforted them, he preserved and protected them, he fed their bodies and nurtured their souls, he guided them and gave them a land they could call their own. And, "when the time had fully come, God sent forth his Son, born of a woman, born under the law . . . so that we might receive adoption as sons" (Gal. 4:4–5). The process, culminating in the act of reconciliation, begins with God. "God so loved the world," in spite of our sin, "that he gave his only Son," *because* of our sin, "that whoever believes in him should not perish but have eternal life" (from John 3:16). So Phillips Brooks wrote of Bethlehem, the birthplace of the Christ-child:

> *The hopes and fears of all the years*
> *Are met in thee tonight.*

In Luke's telling of the publican's desire to see Jesus it would be almost natural for us, and for those who witnessed the encounter, to suppose that this whole incident occurred on Zacchaeus' initiative. Not so, as Jesus explained: "the Son of Man came to seek and to save the lost." (It is we who are lost, not God.) The unknown author of these lines expressed it beautifully:

> I sought the Lord, and afterward I knew
> He moved my soul to seek him, seeking me;
> It was not I that found, O Saviour true,
> No, I was found of thee.

In view of the kind of ministry our Lord conducted—healing the sick, giving sight to the blind, raising the dead, restoring the cripple—the possibility of anyone's being offended at him, much less ashamed of him, must have seemed remote indeed. Yet it was Jesus himself who brought the matter up (Luke 7:23, and our present text in Mark's Gospel). It was inevitable that people would ask, "Who then is this?" (Mark 4:41), and as time went on the question was being asked and answered with increasing frequency and urgency (8:27–30). So it was that Jesus "began to teach them" what it meant to be the Messiah and, after rebuking Peter, what it meant to be a disciple (8:31–38). The news was not welcome.

As has been said, there were in Israel many views of the office and function of the Messiah, when he should make his appearance. Some thought of him as one who would recover the prestige of Israel by force of arms; others that he would purge the nation of pagan and alien influence; and still others in terms of a revolutionary who would subvert the power of imperial Rome and set the nation free. All these views held in common the expectation of a public "success." But Jesus said that real victory (in quite a different sense) could come only through the Messiah's humiliation, suffering, and death (v. 31). Having taught the people what victory would cost him, he then explained what victory would involve for them—and for us. It would mean a denial of self, the acceptance of suffering, and the loss of life. No one can pretend that this is easy.

Are you and I ashamed of our Savior because it would be too costly to be proud of him? Do we resent the fact that, far from being a public success, our Lord died on a cross as a common criminal? Are we afraid that

Though I knew his love who followed,
Yet was I sore adread
*Lest, having him, I must have naught beside.**

These are the searching questions that every disciple must answer for himself. The apostle Paul was emphatically not of two minds on the subject. As one who has "suffered the loss of all things," he counts them "all as refuse, in order that I may gain Christ" (Phil. 3:8). Again and again (Rom. 1:16, 5:5, 9:33; 2 Tim. 1:12) he writes that he is "not ashamed" of Christ and his gospel. No disciple worthy of the name could feel other than Paul. This, the price of life, is a small price to pay.

*Francis Thompson: *The Hound of Heaven*

THIRTEEN
THE NEW FREEDOMS

Mark 2:13–3:6 ———————————————— Luke 5:27–6:11

THE PASSAGE OF SCRIPTURE THAT COMES FROM MARK
presents us with a series of events in which some scholars see a
deliberate pattern; that is, that Mark wants us to understand
them *in this order*. The incidents are: the calling of Levi, the
meal at Levi's home, the questions and answers on fasting, the
question of sabbath observance in relation to plucking grain, and
the same question related to healing. The calling of Levi caused
no comment, favorable or otherwise. But the healing on the
sabbath prompted the Pharisees to consult the Herodians on how
Jesus might best be destroyed. There is evidence here of mounting antagonism to our Lord, attributable to the fact that with each
succeeding incident Jesus was making his claim to Messiahship
more and more explicit. To the legalists, he seemed to be flouting
the law in regard to established customs. He introduced a new
sense of freedom under God to which the Pharisees took strong
objection. It may be that they sensed in his attitude a challenge to
their own authority as pre-eminent among the sects of ancient
Judaism. In their view, if Jesus were permitted to teach what he
practiced, only chaos could result.

Jesus used the same words to summon Levi as he had previously used to enlist Simon, Andrew, James, and John (Mark
1:16–20). On that occasion Jesus had evidently been alone and
did not have to contend with the reaction of a crowd of onlookers.
In the present case, however, "all the crowd gathered about him,
and he taught them." Thus Jesus was no longer a solitary itiner-
ant preacher whose impact on the community could be dismissed
as negligible. His activity was beginning to take on some of the

characteristics of a movement. The first four disciples to be called had already become identified with him and had appeared with him in the synagogue at Capernaum. It would soon be a matter of public knowledge that Jesus was gathering a coterie of disciples about him. Although no word of rebuke was forthcoming on the occasion of Levi's call, it may have served to alert the Pharisees to what they believed to be subversive of a proper understanding of Jewish tradition.

A bit later Levi, like Zacchaeus, invited Jesus and the others to share a meal with him. Among the guests were "many tax-gatherers and sinners." The Pharisees asked, in effect, why one who purported to be a teacher of the people would so lower himself as to be found in such company. Our Lord's reply has become a classic: if a doctor mingles only with healthy people he is not doing his job, which is to cure the sick; similarly, if the Messiah consorts only with righteous people he will have no opportunity of inviting sinners (to the Messianic banquet, a common metaphor for the kingdom of God). Thus did Jesus understate his claim to be the Messiah; but the Pharisees would not miss or overlook the significance of his words. As it belongs to the office and function of a physician to be in the company of his patients, so it belongs to the office of the Messiah to consort with those who need him.

The disciples of John the Baptist had entered upon a period of fasting, as had the Pharisees and their disciples. Jesus and his disciples did not follow suit, as might be expected of those who were truly concerned for the kingdom of God. People began to ask for an explanation.

There is in Scripture no word of God by which men and women are commanded to fast in obedience to him. There are, however, many instances of unprescribed fasting, public and private. Private fasting may indicate remorse and supplication, as in David's case when asking for the life of the child born to him by the wife of Uriah (2 Sam. 12:22). Public fasting occurred from time to time in connection with common guilt (e.g. 1 Sam. 7:6). In the days of Zechariah there were stated commemorative fasts on the fourth, fifth, seventh, and tenth months (Zech. 8:19). In the New Testament Anna served the Lord with fasting (Luke 2:37), and the Pharisees fasted twice a week (Luke 18:12). Fasting was therefore a voluntary form of discipline for which no single reason was adduced. It might signify humility, remorse, commemoration, mourning, sorrow, and sometimes (mistakenly) righteousness.

Whatever the occasion, a period of fasting is a period of austerity. Accordingly, with Jesus present among them, it was no time for his disciples to engage in a fast. For Jesus to decline food almost at the very moment that he was inviting people to attend a (Messianic) banquet would be an exercise in self-contradiction. The kingdom of God is often likened to a feast (Matt. 8:11) or a marriage feast (Matt. 22:2, 25:10), during which guests are not normally asked to abstain. (The early Christians frequently used the marriage relationship to illustrate the relation between Christ and the church. See especially 2 Cor. 11:2; Ephes. 5:23–33; Rev. 19:7ff, 21:9.)

Jesus and his disciples are free to abstain from fasting; in their circumstances, fasting would be quite out of place. The new age, the kingdom, has already dawned, its initiator is in their midst, and the keynote of that event is joy, not sorrow. It is a further implied, unspoken claim made by Jesus to be the Messiah.

The day on which Jesus and his disciples were found going through the grain fields was a sabbath day; i.e. a seventh day, and therefore Saturday. It was the day "to remember," to keep holy, and not be defiled with work. "The Lord your God" rested on the seventh day of creation, and as his children you should do the same. In fact, you *show* that you are his children by doing as he did (see Exod. 20).

In the New Testament the sabbath day is mentioned nearly sixty times, without exception referring to the Jewish sabbath— the seventh day of the week. (The only references to the first day of the week, our Sunday, are in the resurrection narratives and the Book of Revelation.) Who then is he who considers himself at liberty to "break" the law of sabbath observance while that law remains in force? The answer is two-fold: conflict exists here between the requirements of human necessity and the demands of the law; Jesus did not hesitate to minister to the former in direct contravention of the latter. People are of more importance than ritual observance of ceremonial law.

Remembering also that the law of the sabbath was a creation

ordinance commemorating God's rest after the completion of his labors, let us go to other sources in the New Testament for an answer to our question.

In the first chapter of the Gospel of John, we are told that God's Word was with him in the beginning, and that God's Word was in fact God. We learn in the same chapter that "the Word became flesh and dwelt among us." Of this Word it is said that "all things were made through him," and "without him was not anything made that was made." These statements are uniformly confirmed in the epistles, which declare that there is "one Lord Jesus Christ, through whom are all things and through whom we exist"; that "all things were created through him and for him"; and that in these last days God has spoken to us by a Son "through whom he also created the world" (1 Cor. 8:6; Col. 1:16; Heb. 1:2). Accordingly, he who stood before the Pharisees charged with violating the law of sabbath observance was none other than he in whose honor sabbath observance was originally decreed. Now obviously, this is either the truth or it is blasphemy. The Pharisees judged it to be blasphemy, and were prepared to have him killed.

It is worth noting here, if only in passing, that to some degree those things which Jesus claimed for himself he extended also to his disciples. We think particularly of his absolving his followers from the charge of breaking the law by plucking grain on the sabbath. (David ate the Bread of the Presence "and also gave it to those who were with him.")

Clearly these selections from the Gospels of Mark and Luke show that, hand in hand with the coming of the new age, the creation of the "new man," and the emergence of the "new creation," there goes also a new freedom. As we find in 2 Corinthians 3:17, freedom is to be found where the Spirit of the Lord is. Curiously enough, this new freedom bears a strong outward resemblance to bondage. Paul frequently speaks of himself as Christ's servant or slave (the same word in Greek), and in other places as a prisoner of or for Christ (Ephes. 3:1, 4:1; 2 Tim. 1:8). Yet it is precisely within this "bondage" that the Christian finds perfect freedom. In being and becoming a child of God, the believer achieves maturity and personal responsibility.

Sabbath observance is no longer an issue for Christians (with the single exception, so far as we know, of the Seventh-day Adventist Church), and has not been since New Testament times (Col. 2:16f). Christ is the fulfillment of the law for us; in him we are free from the law. Christians therefore abandoned the seventh day as a commemorative observance and began to meet together on the first day of the week—turning, as it were, from the "old" creation to the "new." It was called, appropriately enough, "the Lord's Day" (Rev. 1:10), signifying the day on which Christ rose from the dead. Sunday ought not to be regarded as "the Christian sabbath" (which the writer believes to be a contradiction in terms), but the church's weekly celebration of Jesus' resurrection from the grave. Sunday is the day on which Jesus asserted and demonstrated his complete mastery of and victory over the powers of sin, death, and the devil; a day of incomparable triumph and unrestrained rejoicing, a day when "the old, old story" is rehearsed again and again in prayer, praise, and proclamation.

And then a funny thing happened. The church began to ascribe and apply to the Lord's Day many of the restrictions which characterized the sabbath in the practice of Judaism! Many of us can remember, even in the early years of this century, the prohibitions we were expected to observe on Sunday—shoes shined and meals prepared on Saturday; the banning of all but sacred music in some homes; the proscription of all reading material with the exception of religious literature. These and other restrictions were deemed essential to the proper observance of the Lord's Day. How different things are now! When speaking of the changes that have taken place, many people account for it by such contrasting words as "old-fashioned" and "modern," or "obsolete" and "up-to-date." Yet the truth is that all the while we have had this freedom because Christ has made us free.

*   *   *

When Jesus said (Matt. 10:29) that not a sparrow falls to the ground without God's knowledge of it, and that "even the hairs of your head are all numbered," he may have been using a figure of speech, but he was also stating a profound truth: God knows and cares. When Jesus withstood the criticism of the religious leaders for having eaten with publicans at Levi's table, he was putting people ahead of accepted custom. When, though opposed by his disciples, he commanded that children be permitted to come to him (Luke 18:16), he was demonstrating that even they are not outside the range of the Father's love. When he paused to speak at some length to the woman of Samaria who had had five husbands (John 4:7ff), the depth and breadth of his compassion for even the most dubious members of the human race was apparent.

In the context of Christian faith, to be a person means to be one for whom God, in the perfect freedom of his own will, and out of sheer love for his creatures, sent his Son. He did so "without partiality" (Acts 10:34), and no one is excluded. What is taught in the Gospels through the words and acts of Jesus about the universality of the "good news" is confirmed and emphasized in the letters (1 Cor. 12:13; Gal. 3:28; Col. 3:11).

The Gospels record uncounted numbers of acts of mercy performed by Jesus, and many more are referred to but not related (e.g. Mark 1:32–34). It is evident that Jesus' mission was to people, that his primary concern was people, and that in his ministry people were his first priority. And it was for them (us) that ultimately he gave his life.

Men and women (and children, too) take on a new dignity and a new importance in the light of the gospel. Only God's own majesty and honor surpass that of his creatures (Luke 19:46). In sorting out and establishing our own evaluations, appraisals, priorities, and standards of importance, let us think of these things as we move in and out among our fellows in the daily round of life.

FOURTEEN
UNSELFISH SERVICE

Mark 10:35–45———————————————————— Luke 10

IN APPROACHING THE PASSAGE FROM MARK SELECTED FOR
our attention in this chapter, it would be well to include in the
sequence, as do several commentators, the preceding verses (32–
34). When this is done, additional emphasis is given to Mark's
apparent intention, namely to make it abundantly clear that the
disciples have missed the point of Jesus' teaching. This interpretation is confirmed by Jesus' words in v. 38.

Before undertaking to expound the gift of "unselfish service," let us first try to redefine and rehabilitate certain words
and phrases in the English language whose meanings have become distorted, having acquired overtones of disparagement. It
needs scarcely to be said that our Lord spent a major part of his
ministry in the performance of helpful and healing acts; nor can
it be denied that the Christian is enjoined to engage in works of
compassion and mercy (e.g. Gal. 6:10). How does it happen then
that the phrase "do-gooder" is, in our vernacular, a term of
opprobrium? And that the attribution of the expression, "a bleed-
ing heart," is in effect a sneer? It is evident that something of a
quite serious nature has gone wrong with the use of the language
at our disposal. Given this abuse of English, Jesus' works of
compassion would have to be dismissed as the products of poor
judgment and misdirected sympathy.

We make these observations so that we may understand at
the outset one aspect of the consequences of our being and becoming followers of Jesus Christ. The natural selfishness of human
beings encourages them to speak disparagingly of concern for

others. On the other hand, ridicule is a small price to pay for the privilege of being numbered among his company.

Since the church militant (i.e. the church on earth) is of necessity a corporate organized structure, it is possible for men and women to "get to the top." A propensity for self-aggrandizement is not unknown, even in the church. Although it is commendable that Christians may wish to excel (in their capacity as disciples), their desire to be *recognized* as excelling is, at the very least, questionable. And to use the church as a stepping-stone to public esteem is beyond contempt.

It was doubtless something of this nature that motivated James and John to ask Jesus for future eminence in the kingdom of God; and it is a source of wonder that Jesus responded as gently as he did. He asked about their willingness to suffer, to "be baptized with the baptism with which I am baptized." The figure of baptism is used in this instance to express the image of being hopelessly engulfed (see Ps. 42:7, 43:2, 69:2). Upon receiving an affirmative answer, Jesus put an end to the matter: such a decision was not his to make.

By way of expounding the nature of the kingdom of God, and pre-eminence therein, Jesus offered the inverse figure of secular life in which "the great man" exercises authority over the people, extracting service from them. It is not so in the kingdom of God. The "first" in the kingdom is the one who serves, not the one who is served. "The more excellent way," according to Paul, is not that of desiring many gifts, but of single-minded love (1 Cor. 14:27ff and 15). In this respect as in many others, God's kingdom is not only unusual, it is unique.

In common with every good workman, Jesus did not ask more of others than he was willing to give of himself. If we should be required to "drink the cup" of suffering (see Isa. 51:17, 22; John 18:11b), he has already done so. If we should find ourselves hopelessly engulfed, it is no more than was required of him.

We are free, of course, to adopt Jesus as an example, and to view his life as a pattern of good works. We may even draw inspiration from knowing what he did. Yet, as was observed earlier, the mere following of an example can be a pretty sterile thing. It need have no vitality within itself. Rather, the sense of

Scripture bears first of all on the kind of person you are—or have become in faith in Jesus Christ—which, in turn, determines what you are likely to do. Paul wrote in the first Corinthian letter (2:16) that "we have the mind of Christ"; and he urged the Philippians (2:4f) to "have this mind among yourselves" the better to "look not only to (their) own interests, but also to the interests of others." In the latter passage the apostle went on to proclaim the extent ("even death on a cross") of Jesus' unselfish service. No enunciating of principles or following of examples would induce us thus to serve the Lord. When in 1415 John Huss gave his life in fiery martyrdom, he did not do so as one following a pattern but in the manner of one following a conviction.

When we contemplate the possibility of using examples of unselfish service other than Jesus, ancient or modern, we are confronted with a different kind of problem: all such examples are human, and therefore imperfect. The selection of an example (hero, idol, or even a leader) can result in later disillusionment, and ultimately in repudiation. Unselfish service has its origin in the spirit rather than in the mind or will.

In Luke's reference (ch. 10) to Jesus appointing "seventy others," we are probably intended to understand seventy other than the Twelve (disciples). They were sent out to precede him in towns and villages to which he himself would eventually go. Their mission was therefore of a preparatory nature; they did not constitute a permanent, coherent body. After their assignment had been completed and their report received, we do not hear of them again.

Theirs was a three-fold task: to pronounce a blessing ("Peace be to this house"), to heal the sick, and to proclaim the kingdom; that is, to exercise and demonstrate the powers of the new age in the service of the people.

Historical parallels abound. As Israel (Deut. ch. 1) journeyed from Mount Horeb to the border of the Promised Land, so Jesus and his disciples travelled from the Mount of Transfiguration to Jerusalem. Moses appointed twelve princes over the people (Num. ch. 1); Jesus had chosen twelve disciples. Moses later selected seventy elders to assist him (Num. 11:15ff); Jesus appointed seventy messengers to "go into every city and place" before him. (According to Jewish reckoning there were seventy nations in the world: Gen. ch. 10.)

The seventy returned, reporting with joy that even devils were subdued in Jesus' name. Jesus interpreted this as confirmation of the validity and purpose of his mission, and of ultimate victory in it. Evidence that this had been accomplished by the power of God rather than by the ingenuity of men lies in the fact that "babes" (i.e. disciples, neophytes) had been employed. Jesus' words here bear a striking resemblance to those of Paul in 1 Corinthians 1:21. The "wise and understanding" may mean professional students of the law (scribes, Pharisees, and lawyers); babes are the academically unlearned whose only distinction lies in their having been called.

To understand Jesus' teaching about service, we need to take a good look at his famous parable of the good Samaritan.

We ought not to think of the man who "stood up to put him (Jesus) to the test" as a lawyer in modern terms. We have today a variety of kinds of lawyers unknown in biblical times: criminal lawyers, civil lawyers, specialists in corporate law, in constitutional law, in maritime law—and a host of others. The man who challenged Jesus was one well versed in the law of Moses, and he was trying to find out how well Jesus understood it. In reply, Jesus himself used the interrogative method and was assured that the lawyer had all along known the answer to his own question: eternal life is promised to those who love God and their neighbor. In order to justify himself in asking so rudimentary a question, the lawyer carried the subject a step further: "Who is my neighbor?" or, "Who is it that I am to love as I love myself?"

The story that Jesus told involved three principals other than the victim: a priest, a Levite, and a Samaritan. It may be assumed that the priest and the Levite were Jews and therefore compatriots of the man who lay prone ("half-dead") by the roadside. Both of them "passed by on the other side," doubtless because they took him for dead and were afraid to risk ceremonial defilement by touching the corpse (Num. 19:11–22). Of the three, the Samaritan (who was outside the circle of orthodox Judaism) qualified as a neighbor to the man who fell among robbers.

The word "neighbor" is normally used to denote someone

who lives nearby. The people who live next door may, in popular speech, be "good" neighbors or "poor" neighbors. Jesus, however, redefined the word and expanded its range of application. In this reinterpretation, neighborliness had nothing to do with distance or proximity. (Samaria was some thirty miles from Jerusalem.) It is independent of shared religious views, common racial origins, and political allegiances. It does not presuppose, but may lead to friendship. Its sole basis is the love of humanity. The celebrated Jewish scholar, C. G. Montefiore, writes of the good Samaritan in these terms:

> The parable is one of the simplest and noblest among the noble gallery of parables in the Synoptic Gospels. Love, it tells us, must know no limits of race and ask no enquiry. Who needs me is my neighbor. Whom at the given time and place I can help with my active love, he is my neighbor, and I am his. (*The Synoptic Gospels*, 2nd ed.; London: Macmillan, II, 468)

In the conversation between Jesus and the lawyer who questioned him, there was no difference of opinion on the central issue: to inherit eternal life one must love God completely and one's neighbor unselfishly; i.e. with all the zeal we would employ if our own well-being were at stake. The two—love of God and love of neighbor—though not identical, are inseparable. Either without the other is incomplete, truncated, and foreshortened. In a context which is only slightly different, James says that a profession of faith in God without a corresponding concern for one's neighbor is a corpse (Jas. 2:17). John points (1 John 4:20f) to the vanity of claiming to love God while being indifferent to the welfare of a brother, and concludes, "this commandment we have from him, that he who loves God should love his brother also." The nineteenth-century hymn-writer Edwin Hatch has caught something of the spirit of this obedience in his "Breathe on Me, Breath of God" with these words:

> *That I may love what Thou dost love,*
> *And do what Thou wouldst do.*

To love "what Thou dost love" is certainly, among other things, to love people; for he so loved them that he gave his only Son.

The gift of unselfish service to people is a matter of such vital importance, not only to the personal life of the professing Christian, but to the corporate witness of the church in and for the community, that it merits much more detailed consideration than we can give it here. It is unquestionably *the* neglected gift of the church. In a generation characterized by almost morbid interest in the disciplines of psychology and sociology, particularly among young people, the church seems blithely to assume that everyone already knows how (and is willing) to help his or her neighbor. And this situation prevails at a time in our history when the strains on human relationships and on the social fabric generally are almost unprecedented in their subversive power.

Briefly then, how does one go about expressing one's love for one's neighbor in practical ways? We venture to submit the following guidelines only with considerable trepidation:

(1) In conscious obedience to the Lord's command to do so.

(2) In self-giving rather than self-seeking love.

(3) In such a manner as to preserve and enhance the dignity of the neighbor.

(4) As one who is fully aware of being the recipient of God's love.

(5) Quietly, unobtrusively, without public acknowledgement.

(6) Without a trace of the "Lady Bountiful" complex.

(7) According to the neighbor's need.

(8) Without the slightest intention of making the neighbor over in one's own image.

(9) Without any sense of personal pride or assumption of superiority.

(10) With genuine gratitude to God for the privilege.

FIFTEEN

PRAYER

Luke 11:1–13; 18:1–14

JESUS' FONDNESS FOR TEACHING IN PARABLES IS WELL known. Accordingly, a definition is offered: "A parable is truth told in story form." A parable thus consists of two elements: the story itself, and the truth it is intended to convey and illuminate. Although the lines of distinction between the parable and other figures of speech are not always well defined, a parable is usually a story, as distinguished from a metaphor or a simile which are phrases or sentences. "You are the salt of the earth" is a metaphor; "As a father pities his children, so the Lord pities those who fear him" is a simile. In the two parables before us (Luke 18:1–14) the evangelist affords introductions (vv. 1 and 9) to inform us explicitly of Jesus' purpose in telling them.

Many commentators are quick to point out that the description of the judge (vv. 1–8) in no respect fits or applies to God; yet the connection between God and the judge is implicit in the parable (n.b. vv. 6f). It is therefore possible to see in the description of the judge the most brilliantly apt and illuminating "description" of God imaginable—particularly with regard to God's freedom. God need have no fear, and certainly no fear such as from time to time assails his creatures—the fear of God. Neither is he under any obligation to "regard" man. He is not answerable to a superior authority—whether person or law—for his attitude toward and his treatment of mankind. That he does regard man (in this case, a woman) is a matter of sheer grace (v. 8a). The passage 1–8a is a sort of playlet written for our encouragement in prayer, depicting how God's apparent indifference to our needs contrasts with the reality of his love and concern.

There are few of us indeed who have not sustained disappointments in prayer comparable to that of the widow in the parable. On some occasions the burden of our prayer has been a matter of the deepest personal anguish of heart and agony of spirit. We ask, we implore, and finally in desperation we *demand* that God answer our prayer in exactly our terms. Failing that, we lose heart and cease to pray. To cease to pray is to cease to believe in God, which is precisely what Jesus does not want to happen.

In this parable Jesus is saying that God does in fact hear our prayers and he answers them. Appearances to the contrary notwithstanding, God will "vindicate them (his elect) speedily" (v. 8). The word "vindicate," to describe the substance of the widow's prayer and God's response to it, is a happy choice. It is sufficiently comprehensive to allow for the possibility and the frequent reality that God wisely does not always grant us what *we* want. And occasionally we are permitted to see, in retrospect, that what he has given us is infinitely to be preferred to what we asked for.

Properly speaking, prayer always takes place in the context of personal faith; and faith does not mean believing in the so-called "power of prayer." The power of prayer is neither the object nor the substance of Christian faith. On the contrary, it is an essentially humanistic phrase expressing some imagined capacity of the individual to grapple with and surmount his own problems by means of a particular discipline or technique. Prayer, as Jacques Ellul has pointed out, is primarily an act of obedience, not an instrument at our disposal. The object, content, and substance of Christian faith is God and God alone. Thus we may regard the second part of v. 8 as "the punch line" of Jesus' story. The Greek word for faith is definite, and the probable meaning is "the true faith." That is, when the Son of Man comes, will he find men and women continuing in prayer, hoping in God?

Because many of the narratives in the Gospels cast a highly dubious light on the sect of the Pharisees, and because they were so frequently the object of rebuke by Jesus (notably Matt. 23:13, 23, 25, 27, 29), it would be easy for us to conclude that they were in every respect reprehensible. And so often is the tax-gatherer shown in a favorable light (Matthew, Zacchaeus, and the present anonymous publican-at-prayer), that we could be misled into believing that there was something inherently admirable about being a publican. Nothing, in either case, could be further from the truth. The extent of the publican's perfidy (in the collection of taxes) has already been noted. It remains to say that the Pharisees were, at great pains to themselves, a conspicuously "good" people. It was their view that the Torah (law) must be kept rigidly and meticulously in all spheres of life; and they set themselves apart from others in keeping with their genuine desire for holiness. Over the years their exposition of the law became what Bornkamm has called "a detailed technique of piety to which Jesus'... message stands in sharp contrast." Jesus clashed repeatedly with the Pharisees, not because they were "bad" people but because their very goodness, legalistic as it was, obscured for them the gospel of grace.

Everything in Jesus' story is calculated to emphasize the contrast between the respective attitudes of the two men: pride and humility. An alternative and very attractive arrangement of the words describing the Pharisee: "The Pharisee stood by himself, and prayed thus..."; i.e. separated from the main body of worshipers. Knowing nothing of grace, he immediately began to recite his virtues. He made a slashing attack on his contemporaries, and a personal attack on a fellow-worshiper. Poor man—his conception of worship was to tell God what a good fellow he was.

> ... is there dialogue if the two parties are in such agreement that there is nothing to say?... What meaning does prayer have if it is a way of saying to God "I am a wonderful person, because you have made me wonderful?" What is there left here for God to say? Complete agreement means silence.... When Jesus says that the Pharisee returned to his house without being justified, he is saying that his prayer did not share in the dialogue with God, but in the silence of God. (Jacques Ellul, *Prayer and Modern Man*; New York: Seabury Press, 1970, p. 133)

The publican also stood apart, but for a different reason. We instinctively sense that his isolation was self-imposed for reasons of humility. He may even have felt that he had no right to be in the Temple at all. His eyes downcast, pounding his chest in the fervor and intensity of his prayer, the publican cried out for God's mercy.

Let us make two observations here: first, that it is perfectly legitimate for Christians to thank God for their innocence of extortion and adultery, but surely not as a matter of pride; rather of gratitude. Forbearance and continence are to be regarded as gifts of God, and as such are to be received with thanksgiving and humility. Second, the commendable attitude of the tax-collector is not without its perils. It is possible to become proud of one's humility. On this occasion it did not happen, and he received commendation in the present and the promise of exaltation to come.

*   *   *

God has never accepted as permanent and final the estrangement between himself and his creatures that occurred in Eden He has never acquiesced in, or become reconciled to, our alienation from him because of our sin. He sought and relentlessly seeks the restoration of a fellowship once enjoyed. He is not lonely, and he doesn't need us: his desire for a renewal of communication and harmony is an aspect of his graciousness and his willingness to forgive.

In an effort to establish some kind of communication with his creatures, God has sometimes asked questions (Adam, where are you? Cain, what have you done to your brother?). He also proclaims (Behold, I will do ... thus and so), and hopes for a response. Or he gives and takes away (as with Job); and on all these occasions God looks for the response of the man or woman who will enter into dialogue with him. It is the dialogue of prayer; and we are invited and commanded to engage in it.

"Ask," "seek," and "knock" (Luke 11:9) are both invitation and command. "Be given," "find," and "be opened" are promise. From our side this may seem incomprehensible, and impossible of realization. We have (only!) God's word that it is not in vain. God *guarantees* the reality and the validity of communication with him. As Ellul remarks, in the absence of that guarantee our speech would be lost in the void, in nothingness.

Commonly, God's response to prayer does not bring about the precise answer we were asking for. There can be another outcome, another solution; and the one that God chooses is always to be preferred, although at the moment it may prove disconcerting. An illustration may help us to understand this aspect of prayer: A young business executive has been obliged to work late at the office. It has been a busy day and he is hungry. Will he phone home to say that he will be having dinner downtown, or to say that he will be home for dinner but will be late? If he adopts the first course he will go to an established restaurant, choose his meal from the menu, and get exactly what he wants. It is a business transaction. It is quite impersonal; there is no social intercourse, no dialogue except what is required to order his meal, and no fellowship. If he adopts the second alternative he may have no idea what will be set before him; he may even be disappointed. Nevertheless, he knows that the meal, of whatever it may consist, is good, thoughtfully prepared, and satisfying. The restaurant meal is impersonal, solitary, and commercial; the meal at home is intimate, communal, and festive.

Prayer has much more in common with the second alternative than with the first. Like prayer, both options have their origin in the young man's need—in this case, for food. As in the second alternative, in prayer we go to those who are known to love us and put ourselves in their hands with confidence. We go to those who know the things of which we have need before we ask. If the meal, i.e. God's way of answering our prayer, is not quite what we expected or hoped for, it makes little difference in the long run. *What* we asked for, namely the alleviation of our hunger, will be found to have been granted.

The dialogue of prayer fosters and promotes fellowship between God and his people. One might even venture to say that it creates an alliance between them dedicated to a common purpose and objective. One does not therefore ask, seek, or knock, and immediately withdraw from the action of prayer. "Prayer is never made in order to escape from the risk of faith, or to be dispensed (excused?) from doing what God gives us to do. . . . God acts and requires us to act. In the prayer and the promise which is attached to it, we must work along with him" (Ellul, op. cit.).

This is what we may call "participation in prayer"; that is, participation in the action that the prayer implies. In prayer we seek God's help in solving a problem or perhaps in removing an obstacle; in his promise he graciously invites our participation in providing an answer. And this becomes the foundation of a living, dynamic fellowship such as God earnestly desires to establish with all his people.

A custom of rabbinical teachers was to provide a brief, formal prayer for the use of their followers. John the Baptist had done this for his disciples. It is therefore not strange that the disciples of Jesus made a similar request. The abbreviated form in which the Lord's Prayer appears in Luke's Gospel (comp. Matt. 6:9–13 and footnote) is determined by the amount of manuscript support given to the several phrases in the prayer. Though in several instances the manuscript support for Matthew's version is less strong, it is his text that has become enshrined in the life of the church.

The use of the word "Father" to address God in prayer does many things. It establishes a relationship of a personal nature in contrast to the abstractions which characterized the vocabulary first of Greek philosophy, and later of the scientists and rationalists—such labels as a Power, the First Cause, the Unmoved Mover, the Absolute, and others. In it is an inherent sense of affection, of family, of authority, and of strength. It is not a relationship of equals; rather it demands from us an attitude of the utmost reverence. This Father requires his name, and therefore his person, to be hallowed. The opening phrases mean: "May the time come when the holiness of God's Person will be universally acknowledged, and his reign (kingdom) be confessed and obeyed on earth as in heaven." If, as we believe, the Lord's Prayer is both a prayer and the model of all Christian prayers, the word "bread" is both specific and comprehensive: it includes everything necessary for the well-being of the individual—food, clothing, health, shelter—all of them gifts of the providence of God. But man does not live by these things alone. He can truly live only in the promise and presence of forgiveness, given and received. Human nature is frail, and Christians do not invite trials of moral and spiritual strength. Therefore we pray that God will not expose us unnecessarily to areas of temptation. This is a prayer for guidance, protection, and deliverance from sin.

Though the doxology or ascription of praise "for thine is the kingdom . . ." may not have been a part of the original prayer, it is thoroughly consonant with it. The unique pre-eminence ascribed to God early in Jesus' ministry is also attributed to him toward the end of the New Testament era (1 Peter 4:11, 5:11; Jude v. 25; Rev. 1:6) and by succeeding generations to the present day.

SIXTEEN

THE MEANING OF CHRISTIAN LOVE

Luke 15 _____

A CERTAIN POVERTY OF THE ENGLISH LANGUAGE SHOULD BE
observed in the area of our study. Our theme on this occasion is a
love that leads to forgiveness, or conversely, a forgiveness that
leads to and culminates in love. In pre-biblical Greek there are
three words, all of which are translated, without differentiation,
by the English verb "to love" and its derivatives. They are:
erao, phileo, and *agapao.* The first of these, *erao,* never appears
in the New Testament. It is the word for sensual love, a power
elevated by the Greeks to the status of a god, Eros. Eros is the
demonic force of sensual ecstasy to which all other powers in
heaven and on earth are said to be inferior. The second word,
phileo, and its derivatives, occurs eighteen times in the Gospels
and Letters. It means liking or caring—the love of friend for friend;
hence *phileo* + *anthropos* = philanthropy: the love of people.
Agapao, and its noun *agape,* by contrast signify a definite purposeful act of will, consciously chosen by the individual. Whereas
eros seeks the satisfaction of its hunger for life in, and at the
expense of others, *agape* suggests kindness, practical generosity,
and the service of others. Striking is the fact that the noun *agape*
is hardly used in pre-biblical Greek, whereas the noun and its
verb occur in the New Testament some two hundred times. At a
very early stage in the life of the primitive church, the word
agape was used to describe a meal served in connection with the
Lord's Supper—i.e. a love feast.

The story commonly known in Christian circles as the parable
of the Prodigal Son arose from a remark made by the Pharisees
and scribes (Luke 15:2) that Jesus received and ate with sinners.

Three parables follow: the lost sheep, the lost coin, and the lost son. The main point of all three is the same: God will go to any lengths to retrieve and redeem his own who have strayed or been mislaid. All three stories end on a note of rejoicing in the restoration.

An obvious characteristic common to Jesus' first two stories is their simplicity. They are also true to life. One has only to read the "Lost and Found" column of a daily newspaper to discover the irrational lengths to which animal lovers will go to retrieve a lost pet. Often the reward offered far exceeds the market value of the animal. And who in full command of his senses would leave ninety-nine sheep alone "in the wilderness" to pursue a single stray? Only God could pull it off. Or again, it would have been more economical for the woman who lost a coin (sixteen cents) to go about her household duties than to turn the house upside down in search of it. She had nine others, and the mislaid currency would doubtless turn up in the normal course of events.

These two stories suggest that every sheep missing from his flock, every coin missing from his collection, i.e. every person who remains outside of his community, is a matter of the greatest urgency with God; and that the recovery of such a one is an occasion for celebration.

The third parable is the greatest and most powerful of the three, involving as it does family ties and human relationships of profound depth and understanding. In the first two stories, God's initiative in reclaiming the sheep and relocating the coin is established. Neither can return of its own accord. Repossession in each case follows upon an intensive search. In the story of the lost son the divine initiative is present (note the preparations made for just such an eventuality, vv. 22f), but it is more subtle. It takes the passive form of a father's abiding love which prompts the son's return. It might be months, or even years, before the younger son would realize that he had not returned of his own accord and volition, but that it had, in truth, been his father's love that had drawn him home.

It has already been observed that the word "love" has several connotations. *Erao* translates as romantic loving, *phileo* in terms of affection, and *agapao* as an act of will. The frequently heard statement that "the Bible tells us to love our neighbors, but that does not mean that we have to like them," may seem unduly flippant, but it does point to an important truth. The love here commanded is not a sentiment; it is a decision, an exercise of the will. It culminates in seeking the neighbor's good, in serving, in working for the neighbor's well-being. It is a matter of willing and doing.

When Jesus confirmed the lawyer's answer (Luke 10:28) that the law requires love of God and love of neighbor, he also said: "do this and you will live." Does this mean that the other commandments are not binding, or that one is free to steal and to covet and to kill at will? Certainly not. "The commandments 'You shall not commit adultery, you shall not kill, you shall not steal, you shall not covet,' and any other commandments are summed up in this sentence: 'You shall love your neighbor as yourself'" (Rom. 13:9). The love that Jesus demands is such that all righteousness is included in it.

It was surely an inspired moment when the apostle Paul sat down to write the hymn in praise of love (*agape*)—1 Corinthians, chapter 13. He did so, he tells us, to show us "a still more excellent way"—the way of love. (It is difficult to understand what considerations prompted our forefathers, in the King James Version of 1611, to use the word "charity." It is *agape* throughout.) One can only conclude that Paul had a thorough grasp of the breadth, length, height, and depth of Christian love. The way in which he describes and defines his subject is confirmed throughout the New Testament, but nowhere else are the attributes of Christian love set forth so briefly and so felicitously.

The singular characteristic of *agape* is that it is three-dimensional. Our love for others has its origin in God's love for us (1 John 4:19f). Christian love is not something that we are able to generate in and by ourselves. On the contrary, if we do not know God we cannot know love (v. 7). Love is the disciplined response of one who has been touched by the Spirit of God (vv. 12, 13).

Love is discriminating—or better, discerning—rather than impulsive. In contrast to *eros*, which finds its satisfaction here, there, and everywhere, *agape* chooses its object and holds to it. Accordingly, "do not choose the world or the things in the world" (1 John 2:15). Love is single (in the sense of the New

Testament phrase "singleness of heart," as in Ephes. 6:5 and Col. 3:22)—it sees only one thing, God *or* mammon (Matt. 6:24). Since serving is loving, Jesus comments that you cannot serve them both. Genuine Christian love (2 Cor. 8:8, 24; 1 John 2:5) is less an attitude than a way of life, a life of obedient service to others (Gal. 5:13, 14; 1 John 3:17, 18).

But what of the man or woman who does not love? There are hints in 1 John that the commandment to love has its dark side as well. To love the neighbor is to be "in the light"; to hate (reject) others is to continue "in darkness" (2:9). A little later the writer becomes devastatingly explicit: "He who does not love remains in death" (3:14b). In short, to love God and our neighbor is what it means to *live* in the light of the gospel.

Neither a sheep nor a coin can respond (i.e. repent), but a person can. One son does; the other does not (Luke 15). We, then, unlike sheep and coins, have a responsibility to requite the love which God has shown toward us. The sheep is returned to the fold; the coin is back in milady's purse; where are you and I? If we are not back in the family circle, the fault is ours.

As the children of God we have a legitimate claim on the heavenly Father. According to Deuteronomy 21:17, the younger son was entitled to one-third of the family's assets. When the prodigal found himself comfortably esconced in "a far country" (which may also convey the sense of being beyond parental scrutiny), his life-style at first was an example of "easy come, easy go"; and in due time he was bankrupt. His desperate need drove him to seek employment, but what his new boss gave him proved far from satisfactory. Driven by hunger and haunted by a sense of guilt, he realized that he had no one to blame but himself. Strangers had no use for him, and "no one gave him anything." To whom could he turn for help? If he went back home, would his father take him in? Perhaps he would; it was worth a try. He could not return as a son, of course; that would be too much to expect. He might, however, be acceptable as a hired servant—just for old times' sake.

It is important for us, in seeking to understand the forgiveness of our heavenly Father, to recognize the humility and genuineness of the son's change of heart. "I have sinned against heaven and before you; I am no longer worthy to be called your son . . ." (vv. 18f, 21). But notice too (in the R.S.V.) that when the son voices these sentiments in the presence of his father, he is cut short without finishing the sentence. Interrupted, perhaps, by the father's anxiety to assure him of a welcome?

The eagerness of the father's greeting and reception of his son was heart-rending and almost pathetic. He could not wait for the boy to cross the threshold, but *ran* to meet him. He put his arms around him and kissed him (as he had no doubt done so often in childhood). And if there is any doubt in our minds about forgiveness restoring the *status quo ante*, vv. 22 and 23 should dispel it. A ceremonial robe signified that the wearer is a guest of honor; a (signet) ring was a mark of status; the shoes were a luxury; and the fatted calf indicated an occasion of celebration—like turkey for Thanksgiving, but more so.

According to Luke's Gospel (11:1ff), Jesus' disciples asked him to teach them how to pray, as John had taught his disciples. Among the petitions that our Lord taught his little company was one for the forgiveness of sins. It is couched in a somewhat peculiar way. With respect to this petition, the major difference is not between the renditions of Matthew and Luke respectively, but between the K.J.V.—to which we have all grown so accustomed—and the R.S.V. The former seems to suggest that our plea for forgiveness from God is made on the pre-condition of our forgiving others. The latter appears to assume beforehand that we forgive others, and in the light of this circumstance, ask for forgiveness at God's hands.

The difference is not as great as it may appear to be. Surely whoever asks to be forgiven knows that he or she is cast upon the mercy of God, and cannot do otherwise than to forgive others. How could we, who ourselves are such great debtors, hope to receive divine forgiveness if we did not of ourselves wish to do this small thing—to forgive those who have offended us? "Let us not settle down to enjoy the offenses done to us; let us not nurse our grudges with pleasure. . . . He who does not have this small freedom (i.e. the freedom to forgive) is not within reach of divine forgiveness" (Karl Barth, *Prayer*; Philadelphia: Westminster Press, 1952).

Christian love—the love that has its origin in the presence and power of God's Holy Spirit—takes many forms. These forms are not, of course, mutually exclusive; it is more a matter of emphasis than of differentiation. We have noted that in one instance (Matt. 6:24) Jesus virtually equated loving and serving. To *serve* is the tangible fruit of the decision to *love*.

There is, too, a love that can offer only comfort and concern. Unable, for circumstantial reasons, to serve in deeds of mercy, this love can only "stand and wait," and in doing so truly serves. (See Milton, *On His Blindness*.) Yet this facet of love is frequently a genuine source of strength to those in need. The simple awareness that there are those who care can be of inestimable comfort and sustaining power to the weak and afflicted, and to those in trouble. But of even greater importance, objectively speaking, is what we may recognize as intercessory love: the love that can only (!) pray. As Tennyson wrote in *Idylls of the King*:

> For what are men better than sheep or goats
> That nourish blind life within the brain,
> If, knowing God, they lift not hands of prayer
> Both for themselves and those who call them friend?

We are acquainted, more or less, with situations involving sacrificial love. In theory at least, there are forms of love which cost us little or nothing. Others involve substantial impoverishment of self in the exercise of the decision to love. An example which often occurs in family life is that of children who surrender their plans, hopes, and aspirations to care for ailing and elderly parents. They may choose to serve to the point of sacrifice, in keeping with the words of our Lord that "greater love has no man than this, that a man lay down his life for his friends" (John 15:13).

But the greatest of these (if we may purloin a phrase) is the love that forgives, because forgiving love costs us more than our service; more than our sympathy and our prayers; more indeed than our lives. It costs us our *selves*, our selfhood, our egos, our humanity. To forgive carries with it the denigration and abandonment of self, and of all that may be claimed on behalf of the self; and this in favor of another. It is truly remarkable that Jesus deliberately chose to go to the cross for the sins of the world. Totally incomprehensible is that he did so with love in his heart and forgiveness on his lips for those who put him there. "Father, forgive them; for they know not what they do" (Luke 23:24). Truly, forgiveness is the ultimate test of Christian love.

SEVENTEEN

THE NATURE OF CHRISTIAN STEWARDSHIP

Mark 12:41–44 ————————————— Luke 16:10–17:10

THE MATERIAL BEFORE US FROM LUKE'S GOSPEL FORMS A remarkable sequence on stewardship, servanthood, and faithfulness in many life situations: the handling of money (16:11, 12), divided loyalties (v. 13), marital fidelity (v. 18), and self-centered possessiveness (vv. 19–31). It had all begun with the parable of the unjust steward immediately preceding. These seemingly unrelated segments of Jesus' teaching are found, on closer scrutiny, to have a common theme which is incorporated in the title of this chapter—the nature of Christian stewardship. In a word, the theme is integrity.

It is possible, and even likely, that Luke arranged these brief, direct sayings as he did in order to minimize the risk of a misunderstanding of the preceding parable. In it, Jesus had commended not the steward's dishonesty, but his prudence.

Our interest is aroused by Jesus' exhortation to be faithful—a call to faithfulness. Our first observation is the stark contrast between faithfulness and its opposite. We are accustomed to thinking of faithfulness in degrees—faithful and (occasionally?) unfaithful. According to the R.S.V., such a way of speaking and thinking is inadequate. The opposite of faithful is "dishonest." Throughout Jesus' teaching, his demand for integrity is strict and uncompromising. This kind of forthrightness is the sort of thing we mean when we say, quoting Aristophanes' *Apology*, that "truth calls spade a spade."

A careful examination of v. 10 is necessary for the very good reason that it is so familiar, so frequently quoted, and so extravagantly misunderstood. It is usually interpreted to mean that a man or woman (boy or girl) who is faithful where a dollar is concerned will be similarly faithful where a sum of ten thousand dollars is involved; and this, empirically, is not always the case. There are people in this world who feel that, for one dollar, the risk is too great and it is not worthwhile being dishonest; but that ten thousand dollars would make deceit worth the effort. Similarly, the second part of Jesus' saying is sometimes held to mean that a person who is dishonest in a matter of a dollar will be dishonest in a matter of ten thousand dollars. And that is palpably not the case either. There are people in this world who might have no qualms of conscience about pocketing an illegal dollar, but who would not dream of absconding with ten thousand.

What, then, was Jesus teaching? As Gertrude Stein might have said, "an honest man is an honest man is an. . . ." Jesus is telling us the kind of people he wants us to be—inherently and scrupulously honest, such that no inducement, however powerful or persuasive, shall affect a change of heart and mind. What that sort of person does will take care of itself. A man or woman of integrity will be faithful as naturally as "a good tree brings forth good fruit." But the tree is a good tree long before it brings forth any fruit at all. And a man or woman of integrity is faithful long before being put to the test.

In this sequence of verses, Jesus speaks in the language of contrasts: "little" and "much," "mammon" and "true riches," "another's" and "your own." He is leading up to every person's crisis of decision: the love and service of money (and all that it implies), or the love and service of God. One cannot be a servant of God *and* a slave to money. Integrity in this context would seem to consist of recognizing God for who and what he is: a good Master and a gracious Lord—to be worshiped, not used; and money for what it is: a highly practical gift and a handy servant—to be used, not worshiped. Christians are expected to be able to distinguish between "the things that are Caesar's and the things that are God's" (see ch. 20:25). Accordingly, faithfulness includes the proper discernment of priorities, so that mammon shall not be pursued, and God shall not be taken for granted.

In their administrative offices the majority of Protestant denominations have a department of planning for "stewardship." In one such denomination the name given to this department is

"The Board of Stewardship and Budget"; and the work in progress has to do with the current and projected financial policies of the church at the national level, vis-à-vis the contributions of individual congregations. It is perhaps unfortunate that the word "stewardship" is used in this restricted sense. Not that it does not apply; it does. But stewardship is a much more inclusive word than its use in this connection would imply. On the contrary, stewardship is an almost omnibus word, covering all aspects of the individual's life as a Christian. It applies to and includes much more than a person's money: his time, his talents, his strength, his intelligence, his judgment—and much more. If the Christian's commitment to Christ is total, then he or she is totally involved, and stewardship obligations know no boundaries.

Although written in another context and for a purpose other than instruction in stewardship, a phrase in Paul's first letter to the Corinthians (4:7) bears directly on our theme also: "What have you that you did not receive?" The proper answer, of course, is that nothing of our own was not given us by God. In terms of wealth and well-being, there is similar recognition of our dependence on the providence of God in the book of Deuteronomy (8, esp. vv. 17, 18). It is couched in the form of a warning: "Beware lest you say in your heart, 'My power and the might of my hand have gotten me this wealth.' You shall remember the Lord your God, for it is he who gives you power to get wealth...." The insight and conviction that all we have and are is from God is basic to our life as stewards.

As the parable of the Talents (Matt. 25:14ff) illustrates, all men and women are not equally endowed—whether with intelligence, opportunity, artistic creativeness, physical prowess, personal charm, powers of persuasion, acquisitiveness, or a hundred other attributes that together constitute the sum total of God's gifts to his creatures. But such as he has given, the faithful steward will lay at his Master's feet in gratitude and obedience. (Note: the talent was a measure of weight used for calculating monetary value, but was never coined.) In the parable the five, two, and one talents stand for degrees of prosperity.

Clearly the concept of Christian stewardship is not limited in its application to what we commonly regard as possessions, i.e. things. And even the use of the word "possessions" in this connection must be qualified. If we are trustees rather than possessors or owners, as the parable implies, it follows that we are accountable for the use we make of this trust.

It truly is difficult to resist becoming enamored of the things we possess. The sleek, high-powered little buggy in the driveway, the beautiful Duncan Phyffe dining room table and chairs, the graceful Queen Anne mahogany drop-leaf table in the living room, the superb combination AM-FM radio, hi-fi stereo, and tape recorder in the den—these and a host of other family and household items put our priorities and allegiances to a severe test. How much easier to count our possessions instead of our blessings—and to see them as possessions. We are in constant danger of becoming the kind of man or woman who, on gaining the whole world, lose our own souls (Matt. 16:26 K.J.V.).

Once upon a time there was a man who perceived this danger and was far from sure that he could cope with it. He had no confidence in his ability to contend successfully with either extreme poverty or great wealth. So he prayed to God that he be spared this trial: "give me neither poverty nor riches; feed me with food that is needful for me, lest I be full, and deny thee, and say, Who is the Lord? or lest I be poor and steal, and profane the name of my God" (Prov. 30:8f). Whereas the temptations resulting from extreme poverty are obvious, crass, and self-evident, those associated with great wealth are subtle, insidious, and sophisticated. You and I can succumb to the temptations peculiar to wealth without ever knowing it. The permissive society is simply an affluent society that has arrogantly asked, "Who is the Lord?" And from the point of asking that question the quality of life is all downhill.

The malignant power of wealth to subvert our worship and service of God is best illustrated by Jesus' encounter with a certain ruler (Luke 18:18ff). The young man appears to have been genuinely concerned for spiritual matters, and particularly for the bearing his conduct might have on his expectation of eternal life. In spite of his impeccable credentials he failed the test because, we are told, "he was very rich."

Our emphasis thus far has been almost entirely on the individual's service and stewardship to God. The story of the rich man and Lazarus (Luke 16:19ff) does not permit us to stop there. The consequences of ignoring the needs of the poor are catastrophic and irreversible.

The story is told in the most vivid terms: a man whose evident wealth was visible to the naked eye, whose diet was consistent with what could be seen; and a man so poor as to have no food, so weak as to be unable to stand, and so feeble that he could not ward off the final indignity—the unwelcome attention of stray dogs. (The K.J.V. rendering is much more emphatic: the "crumbs which fell from the rich man's table"; i.e. pieces of bread which were used by guests to clean their hands, and then discarded under the table.)

Here, then, is a gap. Scripture calls it a chasm, or an abyss. It is a man-made abyss of the most horrendous proportions. Is this word-picture overdrawn, or exaggerated? If we think of the economic and social conditions of, for example, North America and India, or Western Europe and Bangladesh, we may conclude that the biblical story is accurate in its essentials. We might even compare conditions within our own country and come to the same conclusion. The point of the story appears to be that the situation on earth admits of change; for those of us who remain—like the rich man's five brothers—it is not too late. All we need is to be told. But for the rich man himself, the books are closed; the chasm which he created during his lifetime is perpetuated, but reversed, in eternity.

To Abraham's exhortation, "They have Moses and the prophets; let them hear them," we would add the name of Jesus. The obligation to serve others did not begin with Jesus' ministry, but was a prominent feature of Jewish religion. If, however, we would prefer to hear Jesus, then we must listen intently to this parable, to his words on receiving little children (Luke 9:48), and to the final irreversible separation of sheep and goats and the reasons for it (Matt. 25:31ff).

As Paul wrote to the Corinthians (1 Cor. 4:2), "it is required of stewards that they be found trustworthy (faithful)"—both in their service to God and in their service to others.

*   *   *

There are several circumstances which contribute to making the story of the widow's mites (Mark 12:41–44) one of the most beautiful and poignant in the New Testament. As a class, widows were probably the most defenseless and vulnerable people to appear on the pages of Scripture. Jesus had just finished a brief period of teaching in which he had flayed the scribes for "devour(ing) widow's houses." And at that point just such a person put in an appearance in the Temple. The timing could not have been better. "In contrast to the bad scribes who eat widow's property, we have now the tale of the good widow and her sacrifice" (Montefiore).

The "two copper coins" are literally "leptons—a tiny thing," the smallest coin in circulation. When Jesus said that the widow had given more than the others he was not making (or inviting us to make) invidious comparisons, that some gave little and others gave much. The sincerity of Christians cannot be measured by how much they give, in the absolute sense. The fact that the widow gave "all that she had" rules out the element of comparison. The gospel does not invite competition to see who can give the most; it commands that we give all.

We are grateful for the preservation and transmission of this story in the Gospel records. There are many of us who feel that we have little or nothing of value to "put into the treasury." We may take heart, not only from the widow's example, but especially from Jesus' words in commendation of her gift.

The widow who gave two copper coins—all that she had—is a prototype of the Man who gave all that he had.

EIGHTEEN
THE OFFERING

Mark 11:1–11; 14:1–15:41 _____

THE DAYS AND WEEKS OF JESUS' EARTHLY MINISTRY HAD
seen, on the part of his enemies, a rising tide of opposition. Yet
his acceptance by the people had continually grown. It was inevitable that the issue should one day come to a head. The entry into
Jerusalem marks a turning point in the nature of Jesus' obedience
to the Father and of his service to mankind. It is a crucial event in
his self-proclamation as the Messiah (see Luke 9:51).

This event has come down to us in the church with a peculiar
adjective attached: the entry is said to be a "triumphal" entry
into Jerusalem. This man was knowingly delivering himself into
the hands of his enemies; he was on his way to ridicule, torture,
and ignominious death. And that was triumphal? Yes, it was. It
did not seem so at the time, in spite of the wildly acclaiming
crowd and their shouted hosannas. Little did they know what lay
in store for Jesus in Jerusalem (although he had told his disciples). The crowd reveled in the prospective ascendancy of "the
kingdom of our father David"—Israel's golden age reviviscent.
Yet Jesus, with leaden heart, let them have their day of rejoicing; perhaps, later on, they would learn that it was truly a day in
which to rejoice—but for a very different reason. Only with the
eyes of faith can we see the real significance of that day, and the
hidden element of triumph in it. From any other point of view it
was an unmitigated disaster.

Although Jesus kept a relatively "low profile" in his approach
to Jerusalem (as compared, for example, with what might be
expected of an advancing Roman legion), his followers, on later
reflection, would not miss the significance of the presence of the

colt. It was a common idea in ancient times that anything intended for ceremonial or sacred use should not have been used before ("on which no one has ever sat"—Mark 11:2; see Num. 19:2; Deut. 21:3). The whole enterprise of using the colt reflects the prophecy of Zechariah 9:9; thus the claim to Messiahship is reinforced and made explicit. The custom of spreading garments before celebrities was much observed in ancient times as a mark of homage, portrayed in 2 Kings 9:13.

As the narrative approaches the final days of our Lord on earth, the question of firm allegiance to him becomes critical. No more the relatively carefree days of listening to his teaching on the hillside, in the marketplace, or in the Temple. Jesus' enemies are closing in on him (Mark 14:1f), and throughout the whole chapter allegiance has become a matter of life and death.

In these harsh circumstances the incident of the woman's anointing Jesus in the home of Simon the Leper (vv. 3–9) is as refreshing as it is poignant. As some around the table complained, it may have been a waste of valuable ointment; but it was a good deal more than that. As a whole-hearted, exuberant display of faith in and acceptance of Jesus, it has few equals in the New Testament. Jesus' words, "she has anointed my body beforehand for burying" (v. 8), provide us with a clue to the deeper meaning of the incident. If, as we may suppose, the woman had been keeping the ointment against the eventuality of her own death, her action may well have been a visible declaration of her faith in Jesus as her Savior and Lord. It suggests, symbolically, that the woman, knowing that Jesus would die for her, gave the ointment to him because he would need it and she would not.

In any event, faith such as this is exceedingly rare—the more so in an age of unbelief. That Jesus lived in such an age is evident from his words to the Pharisees as related in Mark 7:6: "This people honors me with their lips, but their heart is far from me." And in similar terms on another occasion he said, "Not everyone who says to me, Lord, Lord, shall enter the kingdom of heaven, but he who does the will of my Father who is in heaven" (Matt. 7:21ff). The situation in our own age may be seen as a further case in point, when (as some believe) the church is virtually dying from a chronic case of nominal Christianity. Of one thing we may be assured, namely that if we remain aloof from genuine commitment to Christ we shall likewise find no inheritance in him. It is small wonder then that wherever the gospel is preached, Christians treasure the memory of this singular act of devotion, telling the story over and over again.

The story of Judas' infamy (which comes next in Mark) has been told repeatedly too, but with a somewhat different emphasis. Those of us who find the first incident charming will find the second story intensely repugnant. If Mark's intention was to place acceptance and rejection side by side for dramatic effect, he has achieved his objective admirably. Even the word "Judas" has been retained in our vocabulary as synonymous with treachery of the basest kind. Such, however, is the mystery of evil, that later when Jesus identified his betrayer as one seated with him at the table, not one of his disciples could be sure that it was not he (14·19)

*   *   *

At the outset of his public ministry Jesus had been exposed to the temptation to accomplish his mission by means other than complete obedience to the word and will of God (Mark 1:12f; Luke 4:1–13). At that time our Lord rejected the devil's blandishments out of hand. Doubtless, during his entire ministry Jesus remained aware of the alternatives open to him. Toward the end, with his life at stake, the issue presented itself again—this time in absolute terms.

As William Barclay has remarked, the description of the scene in the Garden of Gethsemane makes fearful (and embarrassing) reading, as though we were intruding on Jesus' private agony. This probably is the place in the New Testament where our Lord's humanity is most powerfully attested. In this crisis he wanted companionship; but not even of all of those closest to him, just Peter, James, and John. The weight of sorrow which Jesus was called upon to bear was such that even death itself appeared preferable. Is there not another way of doing this—of accomplishing the desired end: the salvation of the world? Is this, inexorably, the will of God for me? Jesus took these problems to his Father in prayer.

If we should find ourselves a bit shaken by the apparent

"weakness" of our Lord in the Gethsemane scene, we may reflect on his recognition of the implacable power of death, of its finality, and ultimately of its horror. Not until after the death and resurrection of Jesus could early Christian martyrs face death with a measure of serenity born of the assured knowledge of the resurrection. Again, we remember that, as pertaining to his humanity, Jesus was one "who in every respect has been tempted as we are, yet without sinning" (Heb. 4:15). There is no sin in being tempted, and Jesus did not yield.

In the last analysis Jesus prayed for the continuance of his Father's guidance, and the continued sovereignty of his Father's will ("yet not what I will, but what thou wilt").

When we speak of the importance of prayer in knowing and doing the will of God, we should be careful to distinguish this from a wild assortment of techniques of divination—astrology, necromancy, clairvoyance, fortune-telling, and the like—by which from earliest times humanity has tried to foresee the future. Prayer is emphatically not such a device; it is not, so to speak, divination in its "Christian" form. In the account of Jesus' prayer in Gethsemane there is no record of God having made a reply or giving an answer. God's will for Jesus is made known *in the event*—in the event of the death and resurrection of his Son. In seeking an answer to our questions about knowing and doing the will of God for us, we must look to the same event, confident that our future and our obedience are safe in the hands of him who raised Jesus from the dead. Accordingly, "we walk by faith, not by sight" (2 Cor. 5:17); i.e. because we know God, there is no pressing need for us to know the future in advance.

*   *   *

On the day of the crucifixion of our Lord darkness fell at noon (the sixth hour). Failure has greeted all attempts (an eclipse of the sun?) to establish a natural cause of the phenomenon, but the search continues. Natural or not, Mark clearly understood it as a divine portent and the fulfillment of prophecy (Amos 8:9).

"My God, my God, why hast thou forsaken me?" Scholars are much divided on the significance of these words. Are they authentic? Are they the expression of a genuine dereliction? Are they nevertheless the expression of a genuine *feeling* of dereliction? The conviction of this writer is that all three questions must be answered in the affirmative. Plainly these are the words of the psalmist (22); and the whole psalm is virtually a paradigm of the Passion. Here the prophecy of the psalmist finds fulfillment. Of equal importance is the teaching of Scripture and the faith of the church that Jesus Christ is he "who has borne our griefs and carried our sorrows" (Isa. 53:4a). At the root of our sorrows is our profound alienation and estrangement from God, and by reason of our sin, his alienation from us. What Jesus suffered on the cross in terms of dereliction he suffered for us. We need never again fear abandonment by God; his Son endured it for our sakes.

Jesus' last cry from the cross (v. 37) should be understood, not as a cry of despair or relief, but of victory. The end for which God had sent his Son into the world and for which the Son had constantly striven, had been accomplished.

At the very moment of Jesus' death, "the curtain of the temple was torn in two from top to bottom" (v. 38). It is impossible from the text to ascertain whether the curtain was the one before the Holy Place or before the Holy of Holies (Exod. 26:31ff; Lev. 21:23). In either case (the latter is to be preferred), the incident may be understood as symbolizing the removal through Christ's death of a hitherto impassable barrier between God and mankind. The individual, through the death of Christ, now has direct access to the mercy-seat, unencumbered by his own sin and by cultus ritual and personnel. This represents the significance of Jesus' death for the Jewish world, which laid so much emphasis on the seriousness of sin; the following verse gives acknowledgement of its significance for the Gentiles (Nineham). The centurion—a Roman and thus a Gentile—is deeply impressed by the fact that Jesus died a victor; he believes, and so becomes the prototype of all subsequent Gentile Christians. (Surely the K.J.V. is right and the R.S.V. wrong in the translation of the centurion's words: "Truly this man was *the* Son of God." See the R.S.V. at Mark 1:1. There, the same phrase is translated using the definite article.)

It has often been observed that in the matter of understanding the history of salvation, Christians have a distinct advantage over our predecessors in the faith of Israel's God. We can look back on some four thousand years of history and prophecy, promise and fulfillment, death and resurrection, and bring this knowledge to our assistance in interpreting Christian faith. Many of us, for example, knew the end, i.e. the resurrection of Jesus, before we learned of the beginning, i.e. the promise made to Abraham.

As mentioned above, in Jewish tradition the reality of sin was regarded with the utmost seriousness. That it was understood to be the impassable barrier between the people and their God is evident throughout the Old Testament, beginning with the Fall in Eden, and culminating in the impasse at Babel (Gen. 3–11). There we learn that as a consequence of human sin the way from man to God is closed, and there is no possibility on our side of a return to innocence, that there can be no reconciliation of God with mankind unless and until sin has been dealt with; and, in short, we will not be permitted to attain heaven by virtue of our own efforts. In this circumstance the offender is helpless. He can ask for mercy, but he is powerless to eradicate his own sin. He must await the good pleasure of him who has been offended. This view of the seriousness of sin as an offense to God is uniformly attested in the Scriptures of the Old Testament. (See Ps. 32:1–5, 51:1–5, 61:5; Isa. 59:2; Amos 5:12; and a host of others.)

If because of our sin we have no access to God, there remains only the two-fold question and possibility: is the way from God to mankind open; and if so, will he take it? The answer to both questions, from the covenant with Abraham to the birth of Jesus, is the divine "Yes." That is why, at the births of John and Jesus, in both the Magnificat and the Benedictus the references to Abraham are given such prominence. The history of Israel and the inception of the church are all of a piece.

If that is so, we would expect to find in the New Testament a correspondingly serious treatment of sin and its "place" in the new age, under the new covenant. And so it is. The child born to Mary, whose name was Jesus, "will save his people from their sins"; the wine of the Supper "is my blood of the covenant which is poured out for the forgiveness of sins" (Matt. 1:21, 26:28). Jesus was heralded by John the Baptist as the "Lamb of God who takes away the sin of the world" (John 1:29). It was he in whose name Peter called upon the Israelites to repent and be baptized "for the forgiveness of (your) sins" (Acts 2:38); and of whom Paul preached at Antioch that "through this man forgiveness of sin is proclaimed to you . . ." (Acts 13:38). He wrote later that "where sin increased, grace abounded all the more" (Rom. 5:20); and to the Corinthians that "Christ died for our sins, according to the scriptures." The statement made in the Letter to the Hebrews, that "by a single offering he has perfected for all time those who are sanctified" (10:14), sums it all up.

The impassable barrier between God and mankind has been overcome, sin has been removed, and that which is impossible with men stands revealed as not only possible, but as actual, with God.

NINETEEN
THE RISEN CHRIST

Mark 15:42–16:8 ——————————————— Luke 23:50–24:12

THE TEXTS OF SCRIPTURE NOTED ABOVE FROM MARK AND Luke offer evidence of the resurrection of our Lord, but no "proof." They deal with the circumstances surrounding the burial and the visit to the empty tomb. That Jesus had indeed risen from the dead was a matter of *divine* proclamation: "he has risen, he is not here" (Mark); "Why do you seek the living among the dead?" (Luke). No evidence appears in either Gospel that those to whom the proclamation was made immediately believed it. It is well to remember this. We sometimes forget that the people of Jesus' time experienced the same difficulty we do in accepting the historical reality of Jesus' resurrection. It is not quite fair, to say nothing of being unscholarly, to dismiss the early church's faith in the resurrection on the grounds that the people of that era were primitive, unsophisticated, and credulous. They knew with the same certainty we do that death is final. They were not disposed to believe in the resurrection even if an angel told them. And that is precisely what we learn from our texts. According to Mark "they went out and fled"; according to Luke "they were frightened," and later when the women recounted their experience to the disciples, they treated the whole episode as "an idle tale." Nothing in these passages of Scripture suggests that anyone connected with the death and burial of Jesus was ready and eager to believe that he had risen from the dead.

In these writings we encounter the first, stark intimations of the absolute, sovereign power of the new age. "The last enemy"—as Paul later called death—the final enemy, had been wasted. At the empty tomb, death stood shorn of its terrifying power.

Let us be clear in our understanding of what is meant by "resurrection." Resurrection presupposes death; had Jesus not in truth died, the word resurrection would not have been used to describe the event of the third day. One must not therefore think of the resurrection as though Jesus had "survived" death. In Mark 15:45, the evangelist uses the Greek word for "corpse" which, as D. E. Nineham points out, constitutes a "stark insistence on the reality of Jesus' death." Further evidence is in verse 44: Pilate's concern to know that Jesus was already dead before giving Joseph of Arimathea permission to remove the body.

If one were to ask what place belief in the resurrection had in the early church, the Scripture's answer is quite simply that belief in the resurrection *was* the early church; i.e. that the early Christian community was comprised of those who believed that Jesus had been raised from the dead. Here we note chiefly two circumstances: (i) according to John (21), when the disciples realized that Jesus was dead, and in spite of two post-resurrection appearances eight days apart, the disciples went back to work— fishing. There was nothing else for them to do. But after Pentecost (the outpouring of the Holy Spirit) they began to preach; and the burden of their preaching was the resurrection of Jesus, and of the dead by him (Acts 4:2, 10, 17:18, 23:6, 24:15). (ii) When the time came to seek a replacement for Judas Iscariot, it was thought essential that only those who had been witnesses to the resurrection should be eligible for consideration. We may take it, then, that the resurrection was the *sine qua non* of the church's proclamation, as it is of the gospel itself. This same emphasis is evident throughout the New Testament, as Paul shows clearly in his sustained treatment of the subject in 1 Corinthians chapter 15, and in his Roman letter (4:25). Indeed, according to the apostle, faith in the resurrection is the presupposition of the Christian life (Rom. 6:4, 7:4; see also Phil. 3:10 and 1 Peter 1:3). In short, *no resurrection, no gospel* (1 Cor. 15:13).

When Jesus' earthly ministry was completed and he was taking leave of the eleven disciples, he gave them his commission and his promise: "I am with you always, even to the close of the age" (Matt. 28:20). How can Jesus be present with his church in the period of his physical absence? He had once said to them, "I shall be with you a little longer, and then I go to him who sent me; you will seek me and you will not find me . . ." (John 7:33).

Would the disciples then be alone? No; for "I will not leave you desolate; I will come to you. Yet a little while and the world will see me no more, but you will see me; because I live, you will live also" (John 14:18f).

What "you" see and the world does not see is Jesus' presence in the world. Since the world does not see it, it cannot be seen by the naked eye or by microscopic lens: the discernment of the presence of Jesus in the world must accord with the nature of that presence. Jesus is in our midst in and by the Spirit—the Holy Spirit of God. This is not the same as saying that Jesus is here in spirit, as we sometimes say, "I cannot go with you but I will be with you in spirit," when we mean no more than "I'll be thinking of you." What Jesus did during his earthly lifetime, the Spirit of God does now. "I have spoken to you while I am with you. . . . the Counselor, the Holy Spirit . . . will teach you all things and bring to your remembrance all that I have said to you" (John 14:25, 26); "he will bear witness to me" (15:26), and "he will guide you into all truth" (16:13). The immediacy of Jesus Christ to the believer and his contemporaneity with every age are, then, functions of the Holy Spirit of God. In this way God maintains fellowship with his people, i.e. through his Son, by his Spirit. It is *because* "I believe in the Holy Ghost" that I can also believe in "the Holy Catholic Church" and "the Communion of Saints"; for the existence of the church and the fellowship of Christian men and women are fruits of the work of the Spirit of God (comp. the Apostles' Creed).

*　　　　*　　　　*

The name of Joseph of Arimathea has commanded the respect and esteem of the Christian community down through the ages, and is mentioned whenever the story of the Passion of our Lord is told. Matthew says that he was a disciple; not one of the twelve, but a disciple nonetheless—and that he was rich (comp. Isa. 53:9). Mark confirms Matthew's description with the words, "who was also looking for the Kingdom of God," and adds that he was a member of the council. The inference in Luke's Gospel is that Joseph was not a member of the Sanhedrin in Jerusalem which condemned Jesus, but of the Sanhedrin in Arimathea. He describes Joseph as "a good and righteous man, who had not consented to their purpose and deed."

It was contrary to Jewish law to allow the body of a criminal to hang overnight (Deut. 21:22f); and particularly over the sabbath (John 19:31). To do so would defile the land. It took a good deal of courage to ask for the body of Jesus, thereby identifying himself with a "known" malefactor. But Joseph of Arimathea did just that. He had a great deal to lose. To say, as Mark does, that he was a respected member of the council probably means that he was respected by his colleagues who sat with him as members of that august body. In spite of his being a disciple of Jesus we may suppose that he had gained no prominence in that capacity, for his name occurs in the Gospels only in this connection. His devotion to Jesus was not, until after the crucifixion, a matter of public knowledge. And he was "rich," which may (or may not) suggest that he had more at stake than most in making known his discipleship. Finally, as far as anyone knew at the time, the issues raised by the life and teaching of Jesus were closed. It was all over. There was nothing further to contest. Why then (belatedly?) did Joseph of Arimathea align himself with Jesus and against the populace by asking for Jesus' body? At so great a risk?

Christian faith which gives no evidence of its presence, devotion to Jesus which is allowed to go unexpressed, allegiance to Christ that is undeclared—these attitudes and convictions are of little use in the service of the Lord. We may believe that sooner or later the choice comes to all of us: open acknowledgement, or uncommitted silence. We are reminded of this choice by Jesus himself: "And I tell you, everyone who acknowledges me before men, the Son of man will acknowledge before the angels of God; but he who denies me before men will be denied before the angels of God" (Luke 12:8f). Silence, we may take it, is tacit denial. Joseph of Arimathea, as a disciple, was also a man of courage and character. Requesting the body of Jesus was an act of obedience to the conviction he held; it was his confession of faith.

For many of us, especially for those living on this continent, it might not seem to be a costly matter to acknowledge Jesus. Indeed, it may have been too easy and, as Bonhoeffer might have said, too cheap. In one sense, we seemingly have nothing to lose by professing Christian faith. But this may well be an illusion. Perhaps our temptations to silence are more subtle, less overt, even aggressive. It requires courage to face persecution and torture for the sake of Christ. It requires courage to face ridicule and ostracism in his name, too. Ridicule is no threat to personal safety or material advancement, but it can be embarrassing and highly inconvenient. How often have we consulted our own comfort and convenience in making the decision for or against acknowledgement! True, we cannot all be heroes for the sake of Jesus Christ, and it is improbable that our names—like that of Joseph of Arimathea—will go down in Christian history. But it might be appropriate if more of us took our courage in our hands and acknowledged openly, and even stubbornly, our faith in the risen Christ.

*   *   *

One cannot but be impressed by the rapidity with which the news of Jesus' resurrection spread among the members of his little company. That many who heard the report did not believe it is of secondary importance for the moment. According to all three synoptic Gospels it was at the behest of the angel guarding the tomb that the women told the disciples of the good news. Mark allows a brief period of reticence ("they said nothing to anyone, for they were afraid," 16:8). But in the "longer ending" (vv. 9–20), which many scholars do not attribute to Mark, it is reported that "she (Mary Magdalene) went and told those who had been with him, as they mourned and wept."

We may regard it as entirely natural that the women, after their astonishing experience at the tomb, would hurry to tell others. It would have been very strange if they had not done so. Yet this explanation may not be complete. There are firm indications in the New Testament of a quality *in the Gospel itself* which demands its communication to others. We recall, for example, the experience of Philip (John 1:43ff) who, having newly joined the little band of disciples, found Nathanael and told him. (The name Nathanael does not appear in the lists of the disciples; but he is thought to have been the same person as Bartholomew.) Jesus' remarkable interview with the woman of Samaria at

Jacob's well (John 4:7–30) ended in much the same fashion: ". . . the woman . . . went away into the city, and said to the people, 'Come and see a man who told me all that I ever did. Can this be the Christ?" Similarly, Paul is unwilling to take any credit for preaching the gospel. With him is an inner compulsion to make known to others the message of salvation: "for necessity is laid upon me. Woe to me if I preach not the gospel!" (1 Cor. 9:16). He later explains the need to preach as having its origin in "the spirit of the faith," such that one follows inevitably from the other (". . . we too believe, and so speak. . .," 2 Cor. 4:13).

It is only with the greatest difficulty that we refrain from drawing from these (and other) incidents a rigid principle relating to the communication of the gospel. We would, however, emphasize what was said in a previous chapter about unexpressed Christian commitment. Examples of mute faith are exceedingly rare in the New Testament, as they ought also to be in the church.

*   *   *

The sum-total of our *natural* knowledge of the nature of this life is that it ends in death. Christian men and women do not normally subscribe to the doctrine of the immortality of the soul so characteristic of Greek thought and mythology, and assumed by many of our poets. The substance of proclamation in the early church was resurrection—Jesus' and ours.

The resurrection sequences in Mark and Luke do not contain any references to our resurrection as a consequence of his. Certain acts of Jesus during his ministry, however, suggest a resurrection for us (e.g. the raising of Jairus' daughter in Mark 5:22ff; the restoration to life of the son of the widow of Nain in Luke 7:11ff; and the raising of Lazarus in John 11:1–44); and in much of his teaching it is mentioned directly. We remember his question and promise to the disciples, "In my Father's house are many rooms; if it were not so, would I have told you that I go to prepare a place for you? . . . I will come again and take you to myself. . ." (John 14:2); and "I am the resurrection and the life; he who believes in me, though he die, yet shall he live, and whoever lives and believes in me shall never die" (John 11:25f).

–119–

It was this conviction of the efficacy for us of Jesus' death and resurrection that led the apostle Paul to teach that "God raised the Lord and will also raise us up by his power" (1 Cor. 6:14), and "that he who raised up the Lord Jesus will raise us also with Jesus and bring us with you into his presence" (2 Cor. 4:14). And Peter, writing to the exiles in dispersion, finds the Christian community "born anew to a living hope through the resurrection of Jesus Christ from the dead, to an inheritance which is imperishable, undefiled, and unfading, kept in heaven for you..." (1 Peter 1:3, 4).

Let us make no mistake about it: Jesus could only have died and risen *for us*: he did not have to do it for himself. He *had* eternal life in himself from all eternity.

TWENTY
REASSURANCE

Luke 24:13-35_____

FOR THE DISCIPLES THE EVENTS OF THE THREE DAYS—FRIDAY,
Saturday, and Sunday, culminating in the news of Jesus'
resurrection had been as trying as they were confusing. They
had been stunned by the tragedy of his death; they were bewildered by the reports of his resurrection. It had all happened so
suddenly: "that very day" (v. 13) suggests that there was more
to come, as indeed there was.

Although Scripture is not explicit in assigning a reason for the
journey to Emmaus, we may not be entirely wrong in seeing it as
a withdrawal, even a retreat. The followers of Jesus had been
bested, and they were taking it hard. Disillusionment, discouragement, and despair were written into v. 21. Even rumors of a
resurrection (v. 23), later confirmed (v. 24), failed to stir their
interest or quicken their flagging spirits.

Of paramount importance in this chapter are the twin mys-
teries of *unbelief* and *revelation*. How two men, who were familiar with Jesus' physical presence, who were intimately acquainted
with his teaching, who were presumably steeped in the tradition
of the Jews relating to the Messianic expectation, and who evidently merited consideration as disciples, could fail to recognize
him on sight defies rational explanation. The use of the passive
mood in v. 16 may suggest that "their senses were supernaturally
dulled" (Gilmour: I.B.).

Similarly, no human explanation will account for the disciples'
recognizing Jesus in the blessing and breaking of bread when they
had not recognized his appearance or his voice. The obvious paral-
lelism in vv. 16 and 31a must surely be deliberate; and if so, what

is recorded here of the knowledge of God and the recognition of his Son is God's doing, not our own. We hear echoes of this teaching in Paul's letter to the Ephesians: "For by grace you are saved through faith; this is not your own doing, it is the gift of God . . ." (2:8).

When compared with the mounting sorrow of the last week of Jesus' life on earth (we call it Passion Week), the days and years of his ministry must have been happy ones for both our Lord and his followers. True, the disciples had received some mild rebukes (and some stern ones) along the way: Jesus had declined to allow them to remain on the Mount of Transfiguration where they had begun to do a little daydreaming (Matt. 17:2ff); he had denied two of them the privilege of sitting the one at his right hand and the other at his left when he came into his kingdom (Mark 10:35ff); and his devastating, "Get behind me, Satan," must surely have made Peter a bit uncomfortable (Mark 8:33). But on the whole they had had a close and rewarding fellowship with him. And all of this had culminated in a "victory parade"—the triumphal entry into Jerusalem.

How quickly and how drastically the scene changed! And how swiftly events followed upon one another thereafter—the shameful conniving of Judas, the celebration of the Last Supper, the agony in the garden, the betrayal, the arrest, the denial, the appearance before Pilate and then Herod, the release of the guilty Barabbas (whose chief claim to eminence, like yours and mine, was that Jesus died in his stead), the scourging, the crucifixion between two felons, the mockery, then darkness and death. It is little wonder that the disciples were bewildered, confused, and uncertain. Far from anticipating these events, they "had hoped that he was the one to redeem Israel" (v. 21).

To say that the disciples were in need of reassurance is a monumental understatement. They had nothing—literally nothing—to which to cling or from which to receive a single ray of hope. Emotionally, intellectually, and spiritually, they were bankrupt. They lacked (as we do) the inner resources to cope with so abrupt and profound a reversal in their expectations.

The need for reassurance did not end with the resurrection of our Lord and the revelation of his identity to his followers. The very nature of humanity is to err, to misjudge, and to doubt. It may be, as was so evidently true of the early disciples, that we are buoyed up in faith by hopes that we have misunderstood, and which in the last analysis do not correspond to the promises made to us. Israel, for example, at no time ceased to be the people of the covenant, but they frequently ignored or misconstrued the nature of that covenant. Similarly, the church has never for a moment ceased to be the People of the Way (Acts 22:4, 24:14, 22), yet often we have misunderstood or disobeyed the very gospel that binds us to God and to one another. In such circumstances it is not unusual for us to be plunged into a veritable abyss of sorrow and despair. In an unguarded moment we may even be tempted to reproach God himself.

The experience of the disciples during those fateful three days is evidence enough that they had come to the end of their resources and were quite unable to "go it alone." No more are we alone in our efforts to lead the Christian life as modern followers of "the Way."

*   *   *

There are probably several hundred million people in the world who know *about* Jesus—and considerably fewer who *know* him. The church has always maintained that there is a world of difference between the two. We can possibly know about Jesus in much the same way that we can know about Thomas Jefferson, Napoleon Bonaparte, or Henry VIII; that is, we can be aware of them as prominent figures on the plane of human history. We may acquaint ourselves with their dates of birth, parentage, early training, manner of life, contributions, if any, to the commonweal, and date of demise. But no one living today would profess to know *them*. Yet several millions of our contemporaries claim to know Jesus; to know him personally, and to have almost daily contact with him. Is this possible? It is obviously impossible to relate to Jefferson, Napoleon, and Henry VIII, for they are dead, but entirely possible to relate to Jesus, for "I am the first and the last and the living one; I died, and behold I am alive for evermore..." (Rev. 1:18). As such "he is able for all time to save those who draw near to God through him, since he always lives to make intercession for them"(Heb. 7:25). This—the faith that Jesus lives—is the ground for the Christian's claim to know him.

During Jesus' life on earth his contemporaries could know him just as we know our friends today. They knew his appearance, his habits, his family, the sound of his voice, and his personal characteristics. Paul called that way of knowing "after the flesh," or "from the human point of view" (2 Cor. 5:16; K.J.V. and R.S.V.). But, says the apostle, "we regard him thus no longer."

What do Christians mean when we speak of knowing Jesus Christ? The answer, given quite simply by the writers of the New Testament, is very largely in terms of power—the power of Jesus Christ in their own lives. The words "tendency" and "influence" in this connection are quite inadequate. Paul, for example, is quite content to suffer his "thorn in the flesh" if only "the power of Christ will rest upon me" (2 Cor. 12:9). His whole ministry was made possible and given to him "by the working of his power"—a power that continues "to work within us" in the ministry of the gospel for the glory of God (Ephes. 3:7, 20). A phrase in the letter to the Philippians (3:10) virtually defines the word "know" as it is frequently used in the Bible: "to have experience of" (comp. e.g. Gen. 4:1 *et al.*). That is, to know Christ is to experience the power of the resurrection in one's own life. According to 1 Thessalonians, Christian faith and life is not a matter of words only, but of words attended and witnessed by God's Holy Spirit, with resultant conviction (1:5). The secret of the Christian's strength and stability lies not in him- or herself, but in the gift of God—"a spirit of power and love and self-control" (2 Tim. 1:7).

The difference between knowing about Christ and knowing Christ? It is a little like the difference between grasping both strands of an electric extension cord which has become detached from its outlet, and grasping the same two strands when the connection has been made. In the latter event we feel the current, and know the power, empirically.

The individual Christian should move from knowing Jesus Christ to sharing this knowledge with others. One would not normally expect to find the sequence reversed; i.e. that one who had no particular commitment to the gospel would seek to propagate it. In keeping with the preceding section, it must be emphasized that the gospel is not a quantum of information or of factual data, the acquisition and assimilation of which is identical with knowing Jesus Christ.

It is instructive to notice how much of Jesus' effort is centered on teaching his disciples what discipleship means, what is involved in following, trusting, believing, and obeying him. These men (and women) knew more *about* him than we will ever know; yet they seem, except for occasional outbursts like that of Peter (Matt. 16:16), to have been curiously blind to the deeper meaning of his words and the essential purpose of his mission. Nowhere is this more apparent than in the story of the journey to Emmaus.

In the communication of the gospel, in addition to the teacher's gift for teaching and the learner's eagerness to learn, is what we might call a "third term" which alone is able to make the whole enterprise fruitful. Paul (1 Cor. 3:6) was not merely being modest when he wrote of his own missionary efforts that, "I planted, Apollos watered, but God gave the growth" (K.J.V. "increase"). More than human effort, industry, and talent are required in the successful sharing of our knowledge of the gospel. What distinguishes Christian education from its secular counterpart is precisely this "third term," namely, the active participation of God's Holy Spirit. The New Testament is unanimous that Christian learning is essentially a *creative* act of God in which the teacher is permitted to be God's fellow-worker (see R.S.V. footnote, as above). Accordingly, anyone who is "in Christ" is said to be a wholly new creation (2 Cor. 5:17). The same theme is underlined by the apostle's words in the first letter to the Corinthians, which we may paraphrase as follows: "Though you have countless mentors in the Christian gospel, you do not have many able to father you in the faith" (4:15). The analogy of Christian conversion to natural birth is conclusive in Jesus' own words to Nicodemus: "Truly, truly, I say to you, unless one is born anew (footnote: "from above") he cannot see the kingdom of God" (John 3:3).

Therefore, as Paul observed (1 Cor. 1 and 2), a strong element of folly exists in our undertaking to preach and teach at all, since the success of our efforts lies in other hands. We do this nevertheless at God's express invitation and command, assured that precisely by means of this apparent "foolishness" will God save those who believe.

*   *   *

When Jesus, on the road to Emmaus, had chided the two disciples for their unbelief, he then undertook, beginning "with Moses and all the prophets," to interpret to them "in all the Scriptures the things concerning himself" (Luke 24:27). He began, surely not with the man Moses, towering figure though he was; but with the books of the Bible ascribed to Moses, the first five books of the Old Testament (the Pentateuch), known as "books of Moses" (see caption over each). Most important is that we notice that in this circumstance, that is, faced with doubt and unbelief, Jesus resorted to the *Old* Testament for confirmation of divine truth. Of course he could not refer to the New Testament, as yet unwritten; but the point for us, with both Testaments before us, is that there is a unity of the two, and that they are consistent with one another in their witness to his person and work.

Having come thus far in our reading, we will recognize that Jesus' "beginning with Moses and all the prophets" was not a last-minute innovation on the part of our Lord. It was, rather, a familiar characteristic of his teaching method, either by inference or by direct quotation. In an earlier study we noted Jesus' appeal to the Scriptures in his confrontation with the devil, as his first and only line of defense. Elsewhere (in Luke 9:22 and parallels; ch. 9:44f, 17:25, and 18:31–34) the same method is evident, chiefly for the purpose of preparing his followers for what lay ahead.

The Scripture is no place to engage in speculation, yet the temptation to do so here is almost irresistible. To what passages, figures, concepts, relationships, and prophecies did Jesus refer in his conversation with the two disciples on the way to Emmaus? The fact that no further detail is given than this bare statement, suggests that what Jesus did on that occasion is now the task of the church.

We need not read more into the revelation at the supper table than is written. At this time and place Jesus chose to open the disciples' eyes to his true identity, but he did so in a rather unique way. Even as a guest in the home of Cleopas *he* took the bread, blessed and broke it, and gave it to *them* ! Most of us are familiar with the family wall plaque which proclaims that Jesus is "the unseen guest at every meal." Better: "the unseen host at every meal."

Despite the lateness of the hour, the two disciples hurried back to Jerusalem to share the startling news of their encounter with the risen Lord. In the telling they were forestalled: he had also appeared to Simon. They listened to his story, then told their own. They agreed that, though they had heretofore been "slow of heart to believe," all grounds for doubt had now been re moved. Jesus, in truth, had risen from the dead.

TWENTY-ONE
THE COMMISSION
• AND THE PROMISE

THE FINAL TWELVE VERSES OF THE GOSPEL OF ST. MARK—
16:9–20—are printed in italics in some editions of the Revised
Standard Version of the Bible. This device is intended to indicate
that they differ in some respects from the main body of the
Gospel. The majority of New Testament scholars believe that
these verses are not part of Mark's original Gospel. The chief
reason for their coming to this conclusion is that some of the best
manuscripts available end at v. 8. Other reasons, taken together,
suggest two possibilities: first, that Mark finished his work but
that everything after v. 8 was lost, in which case vv. 9–20 is
probably a later substitution; or that Mark for some unexplained
reason left his work unfinished, in which event vv. 9–20 is a
subsequent addition.

The issue here is simply a literary distinction. Nineham, who
quotes other major scholars with approval, says that vv. 9–20 is
"canonically authentic," that is, part of the canon of Holy Scripture; but not authentic in the literal sense—not the work of St.
Mark. The church's rule here must surely be contained in the
phrase, "canonically authentic."

There are in fact no issues bearing on the nature of the faith
involved in these scholarly observations. Indeed, parts of the
section under consideration appear to be condensations of what
Luke tells us in more extended form. Vv. 12 and 13, for example,
appear to be an abbreviation of the story of the journey to Emmaus; and v. 14 corresponds briefly to Luke 24:37.

Foremost among the questions raised by this and parallel
passages of Scripture is that of the nature of Jesus' body after his

resurrection. Jesus himself invited the question (Luke 24:29) and provided the answer, showing that his body was substantial, as distinct from spiritual or ghostly. The empty tomb is evidence that Jesus' earthly body was raised. His post-resurrection body bore the marks of the crucifixion (John 20:20; the Thomas sequence, John 20:24–28). Yet he vanished from the home of Cleopas (Luke 24:30). On Sunday evening, the day of the resurrection, while the disciples were gathered secretly behind closed doors (for fear of the Jews), Jesus "came and stood among them" (John 20:19); as he did also when they were discussing the Emmaus experience (Luke 24:36), after which he ate a piece of broiled fish. Finally, after promising to the disciples the gift and power of the Holy Spirit (Acts 1:8), he was removed from their sight, to be seen no more.

Clearly the biblical witness is to a bodily resurrection. The Scriptures insist, however, that after the resurrection Jesus' body possessed qualities that had not been evident before his death. It had been subtly and mysteriously "changed" (comp. 1 Cor. 15:51). We cannot say more; we dare not say less.

Our major emphasis in this study is Jesus' commissioning his disciples; the preparatory verses (36–43) are still concerned with the genuineness of his resurrection. This is as it should be: apart from the reality of the resurrection, what would he be commissioning them for? The disciples are to become "witnesses of these things" (v. 48 and Acts 1:8). And later, if the whole world is to know and believe the resurrection, how else can this be accomplished except by the eyewitness testimony of those who were there, who saw and touched him?

An unmistakable feature of chapter 24 of Luke's Gospel is the dogged, stubborn, unrelenting insistence of our Lord on the reality of his resurrection, and on the necessity of his disciples' unqualified acceptance of it as a condition of their discipleship. Accordingly, in both word and deed Jesus' witness to himself is repetitive: he appears twice—once on the Emmaus road and again when all the disciples are gathered, to "stand among them"; twice he withdraws (vanishes)—once from the home of Cleopas, and again from Bethany; twice he takes food as evidence of his post-resurrection corporeality—once in the breaking of bread, and again in accepting the broiled fish; and twice (vv. 27 and 45) he expounds at length on his resurrection in the light of Old Testament prophecy.

Then the assignment of responsibility: "You are the witnesses"; and the gift of power: "I send the promise of my Father upon you." Luke continues and enlarges on this story, and makes it more explicit in the Acts of the Apostles (1:8ff).

One can but marvel at the difference in the attitude and demeanor of Jesus' followers after his first (the crucifixion) and second (the ascension) leave-takings. After his death on the cross they were inconsolable, without hope or purpose, and in complete disarray. Jesus had foreseen that this would be the case. "You will all fall away; for it is written, 'I will strike the shepherd, and the sheep will be scattered'" (Mark 14:27). Our human resources are inadequate and unavailing in coping with death and bereavement. The scene during and after Jesus' ascension stands in marked contrast to the first. It was one of order rather than confusion. The little company may have been a bit wistful (Acts 1:10), but there is no indication that they were sad. They were together—the disciples, the women, Jesus' mother, and his brothers. No bewilderment, no beating of the breast, and no recriminations. Quietly awaiting the gift of the Spirit in accordance with Jesus' earlier instruction, they gave themselves to prayer. They now had a future; accordingly, in preparation for the days ahead, they arranged to fill out their appointed numbers in choosing Matthias to replace Judas. We note here too that, as Jesus had foreseen their broken ranks after his death, he also foresaw their regrouping after his resurrection. "But after I am raised up, I will go before you to Galilee" (Mark 14:28).

Not long afterward Peter was speaking publicly in a manner not unlike that of his Master: "Men of Israel . . . this Jesus . . . you crucified and killed by the hands of lawless men. But God raised him up . . ." (Acts 2:22ff). Does that not sound familiar, almost as though Jesus himself were speaking? And more was to come from Peter, from John, from Stephen, and eventually from Paul. More of what? More preaching of the resurrection, more calling to repentance and faith, more healing and cleansing (i.e. more signs of the power of the new age)—and more opposition and persecution. And so it was that this once fearful and thoroughly frightened little band of believers came out of seclusion into the Temple, the marketplace, and the council chamber to say one thing: "Jesus Christ is risen."

*   *   *

The Christian life is lived in the light and knowledge, and as a consequence of, the death and resurrection of Jesus Christ. It is uniformly spoken of in the New Testament as something new: the resurrection of Jesus affords us an opportunity to "walk in the newness of life" (Rom. 6:4). As Abram, Sarai, Jacob, Simon, and Saul were given new names as a result of their respective encounters with God, so the Christian is given new life in consequence of his or her encounter with Jesus Christ. The essence of that life, objectively observed, is *witnessing*.

Quite clear from all three synoptic Gospels and the Book of the Acts is that originally Jesus gave his commission only to the eleven disciples (see Matt. 28:16; Mark 16:14; Luke 24:33; and Acts 1:13). The special place given to the eleven resulted from two circumstances: they had been called to be disciples; and they had been eye- and ear-witnesses to Jesus' ministry, death, and resurrection. Thus "the household of God," which is the church, shall have as its foundation the testimony of the "apostles and prophets, Christ Jesus himself being the chief cornerstone" (Ephes. 2:20).

The church lives and grows by witnessing to the power of the resurrection, by attesting the validity of Jesus' words and deeds. Members of his body verify in their own lives the truth of what he has said and done. When Jesus said that the disciples would "be my witnesses in Jerusalem and in all Judea and Samaria and to the end of the earth" (Acts 1:8), he was saying that they would be called upon to testify of him and to validate the claims of the gospel at all times and in all places. The commandment, to "make disciples of all nations" (Matt. 28:19), anticipates and authenticates the worldwide mission of the church, and the personal responsibility of its members for their individual witness.

Witnessing to and for Jesus Christ has many facets. Sometimes it may be a simple matter of speaking up, of "acknowledging me before men" (Luke 12:8). But it does not end there. Being a witness in the New Testament sense involves more than our words; it engages the whole person: talents, attitudes, convictions, abilities, integrity, faithfulness, and fellowship. It embraces our *selves*, our egos—what we are and how we live.

Although throughout the New Testament an interest in and zeal for active discipleship is everywhere apparent, we may note that most of our guidelines for faithful stewardship and Christian witness are found in Paul's dictum (Rom. 12:2) that we ought not to accommodate ourselves to the manners and customs of this world, "but be transformed through the renewal of your mind." He makes it plain from the outset that to take our ethical agenda from the world's standards in any age is not a live option for Christians. We are to live rather from the good news of the gospel and its implications for life and conduct, insofar as it is humanly possible. Inevitably, therefore, the Christian requirement for obedience will from time to time run counter to prevailing secular behavior.

*   *   *

It may be profitable for us to consider discipleship from two points of view: as it exists among Christians in their ministry to one another, and as a function of the church in relation to the world.

Within the community of believers there is variety in the types of witness, all of which are manifestations of the Spirit, and gifts of God for the common good (1 Cor. 12:7). Among these, as taught by the apostle, are wisdom, knowledge, faith, healing, miracles, prophecy, and tongues. Within the fellowship the analogy used is that of the human body with feet, hands, eyes, ears, and so on—not one of which parts (gifts) is dispensable. Accordingly, "God has appointed in the church first apostles, second prophets, third teachers, then workers of miracles, helpers, administrators, speakers in various tongues" (v. 28; see also Ephes. 4:11–14). The apostle returns to this theme in his letter to the Romans (12:4–8), where even giving is regarded as a gift of God. By the patient, faithful, and obedient exercise of these gifts within the church, the fellowship is deepened, individual needs are met, the word of God is proclaimed, and the truth purified and preserved.

Jesus once warned his disciples (Matt. 7:16) against being taken in by the blandishments of false prophets, saying "You will know them by their fruits." If we are willing to concede the same insight to others, then the phrase may be used against *us*, too. They (the world) will know us by our fruits, as witnesses to and ambassadors for Christ. Partly, at least, for this reason the New Testament abounds with exhortations to embrace "good conduct among the Gentiles" (1 Peter 2:12) and to concentrate on "what is true, honourable, just, pure, lovely and gracious" (Phil. 4:8). It enhances the glory of God that we bear much fruit and so prove to be Jesus' disciples (John 15:8). The obedient witness will heed Jesus' words in the Sermon on the Mount: "Let your light so shine before men, that they may see your good works and give glory to your Father who is in heaven" (Matt. 5:16).

We need not be ignorant of the things that God requires of us if we would be faithful witnesses for his Son. It is all there in the New Testament. We note such broad exhortations as "Let every one who names the name of the Lord depart from iniquity," and, "I . . . beg you to lead a life worthy of the calling to which you have been called . . ." (2 Tim. 2:19; Ephes. 4:1). The more specific references are there too—so numerous, so detailed, and so explicit as to leave us without excuse.

One further observation needs to be made: all of this—your life and mine as professing Christians—is that men may see and give glory to our Father who is in heaven. The world may or may not (as it sees fit) admire us; but that is of no importance. Paul once wrote (2 Cor. 4:5) that "what we preach is not ourselves, but Jesus Christ as Lord"; John the Baptist, reflecting on the ascendancy of Jesus, told his disciples that "He must increase, but I must decrease" (John 3:30). In this spirit of lowliness and meekness, rather than pride and exaltation, the Christian properly makes his or her witness to the Lord of all.